# Discover Bexley

# Discover
# BEXLEY
## and
# SIDCUP

A comprehensive guide to BEXLEY, BEXLEYHEATH, WELLING, SIDCUP, FOOTSCRAY & NORTH CRAY

by DARRELL SPURGEON

**GREENWICH GUIDE-BOOKS**

Copyright © Darrell Spurgeon 1993

All rights reserved. No part of this book may be copied or otherwise reproduced, stored in a retrieval system, or transmitted, in any form or by any means, electronic, mechanical, photocopying, recording or otherwise, without the prior permission of the author.

First published in Great Britain 1993 by
Greenwich Guide-Books,
72 Kidbrooke Grove, Blackheath, London SE3 0LG
(phone 0181-858 5831)
Second impression 1995

Copies available from Bexley Local Studies Centre, Hall Place,
Bourne Road, Bexley, Kent DA5 1PQ
(phone 01322 526574)

Other volumes in the same series by the same author:
Volume I, covering Woolwich, Plumstead, Shooters Hill,
East Wickham, Abbey Wood & Thamesmead
Volume II, covering Greenwich, Westcombe & Charlton
Volume III, covering Eltham, New Eltham, Mottingham,
Grove Park, Kidbrooke & Shooters Hill
Volume V, covering Crayford, Slade Green, Erith,
Belvedere, Abbey Wood & Thamesmead

Front cover photograph is Hall Place, north front (c1540-60) -
*gazetteer reference Bexley 1*

Printed in England by Biddles, Guildford

A catalogue record for this book is available from the British Library
ISBN 0 9515624 3 6

# CONTENTS

Foreword page 7

**BEXLEY**
Introduction 11
Section 'A' (Hall Place) 14
Section 'B' (Bexley Village) 19
Section 'C' (Parkhurst, Blendon & Albany Park) 28
Section 'D' (Bexley Hospital & Joydens Wood) 31
Suggested Walks 34

**BEXLEYHEATH**
Introduction 37
Section 'A' (Broadway & Crook Log) 39
Section 'B' (Upton) 43
Suggested Walks 46

**WELLING**
Introduction 49
Section 'A' (Falconwood, High Street & Danson) 51
Section 'B' (East Wickham) 54

**SIDCUP**
Introduction 56
Section 'A' (Central Sidcup) 61
Section 'B' (Lamorbey & Blackfen) 69
Suggested Walks 74

**FOOTSCRAY**
Gazetteer 77
Suggested Walk 82

**NORTH CRAY**
Gazetteer 83

Notes on some architects & artists 90
Bibliography 93
Index 94

**MAPS**
Bexley & Sidcup 6
Bexley Sections 'A', 'B' & 'C' 10
  Enlargement of inset 20
Bexley Section 'D' 32
Bexleyheath 36
Welling 48
Sidcup Section 'A' 60
Sidcup Section 'B' 68
Footscray 76
North Cray 84

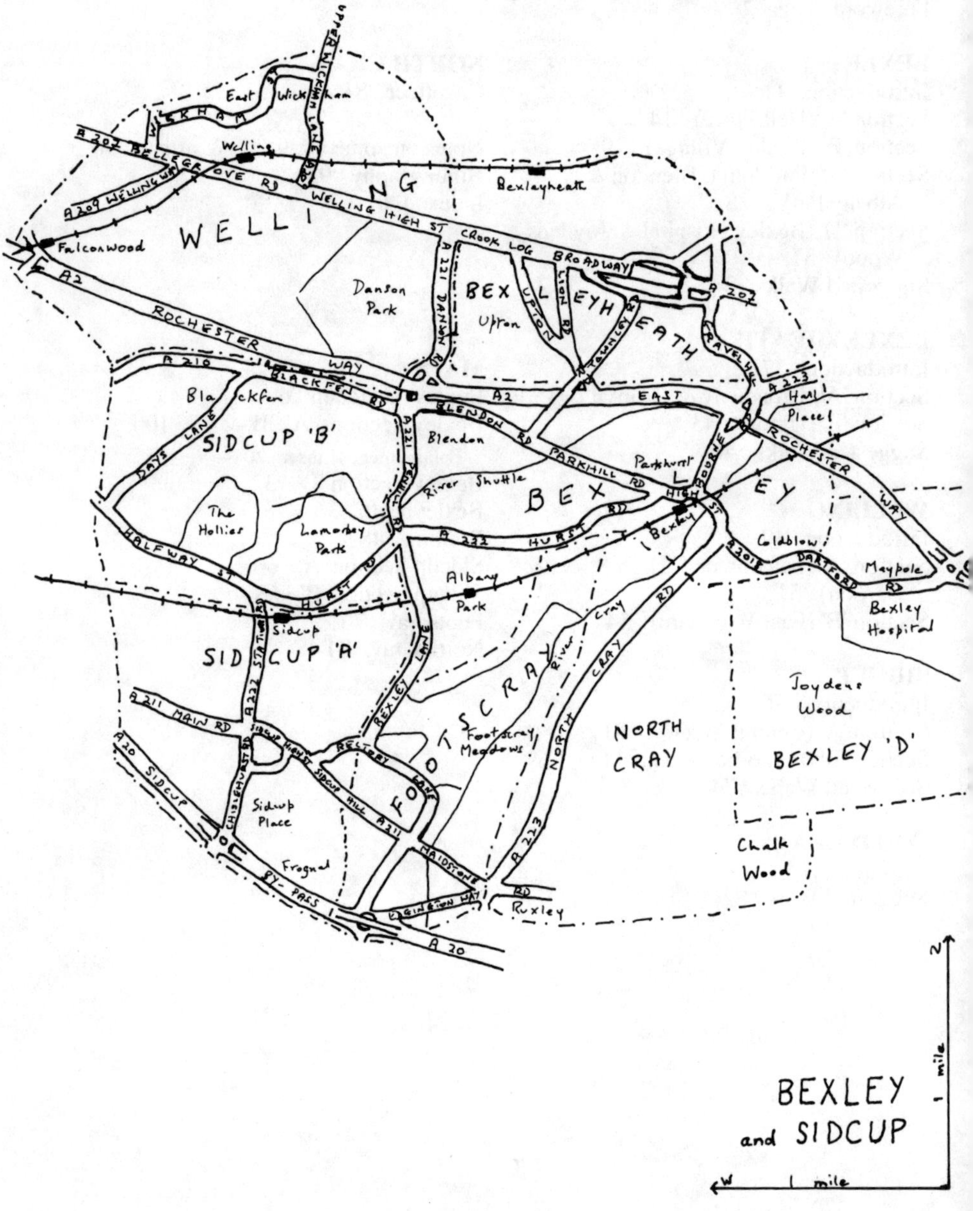

BEXLEY
and SIDCUP
East Wickham
Welling
WICKHAM
A 207 BELLEGROVE RD
A209 WELLING WAY
Falconwood
WELLING
WELLING HIGH ST
CROOK LOG
BROADWAY
Bexleyheath
Danson Park
A 221 DANSON RD
BEXLEYHEATH
Upton
UPTON
LION RD
TOWNLEY RD
A 207
A2
ROCHESTER WAY
A 210
BLACKFEN RD
Blackfen
BLENDON RD
Blendon
EAST
GRAVEL HILL
A 223
Hall Place
SIDCUP 'B'
DAYS LANE
River Shuttle
PARKHILL RD
Parkhurst
BOURNE
ROCHESTER WAY
BEXLEY
The Hollies
Lamorbey Park
A 222
HURST RD
HIGH ST
Bexley
Coldblow
A 2018
DARTFORD RD
Maypole
HALFWAY ST
Albany Park
Sidcup
STATION RD
Bexley Hospital
SIDCUP 'A'
BEXLEY LANE
FOOTSCRAY
River Cray
CRAY RD
NORTH CRAY
Joydens Wood
A 211 MAIN RD
Footscray Meadows
NORTH CRAY
BEXLEY 'D'
A 20 SIDCUP
CHISLEHURST RD
SIDCUP HILL
RECTORY LANE
Sidcup Place
A 211
A 223
Chalk Wood
Frognal
MAIDSTONE RD
BY-PASS
EDGINGTON WAY
Ruxley
A 20
N
1 mile
W

# FOREWORD

For each of the six areas covered by this guide - Bexley, Bexleyheath, Welling, Sidcup, Footscray and North Cray - there is a basic framework consisting of brief introduction, gazetteer, map(s) and (except in the case of Welling and North Cray) suggested walk(s).

The boundaries between the areas, which are topographical (rather than administrative) boundaries, are shown on the map opposite.

This volume overlaps with the section on East Wickham in the first book of this series, 'Discover Woolwich and its Environs'; it is hoped this will not be considered an unnecessary duplication, in fact some of the entries have been updated.

The areas covered by this book are in the London Borough of Bexley, except for: Ruxley (included under North Cray), which is in the London Borough of Bromley; and Bexley Hospital, Maypole and part of Joydens Wood, which are in Dartford Borough, and therefore in Kent not London. Before 1965 all the areas were in Kent - from 1937 Bexley, Bexleyheath and Welling came under Bexley Borough Council; and from 1933 Sidcup, Footscray and North Cray came under Chislehurst & Sidcup Urban District Council.

Each area has one or more maps and a detailed gazetteer. Every location in the gazetteer is identified (using location numbers) on a map. There are also suggested walks, but only where places of interest are concentrated within an area which makes walking practicable and interesting. The walks would be best followed in conjunction with the gazetteers and maps; the gazetteers indicate things to see at each location, and the maps make the route of the walks easier to follow.

Bexley is divided into four sections - Section 'A' Hall Place; Section 'B' Bexley Village; Section 'C' Parkhurst, Blendon & Albany Park; and Section 'D' Bexley Hospital & Joydens Wood. There are three maps - one covering the first three sections, an enlargement of most of Section 'B', and one covering Section 'D'. There are suggested walks which cover most locations in Bexley Village, Parkhurst and Blendon. The gazetteer entry for Hall Place indicates how best to see the places of interest; and the gazetteer entry for Joydens Wood contains advice on walking through the wood.

Bexleyheath is divided into two sections - Section 'A' Broadway & Crook Log'; and Section 'B' Upton. One map covers both sections; the suggested walk covers most locations in Section 'A' and all locations in Section 'B'.

Welling is divided into two sections - Section 'A' Falconwood, High Street & Danson; and Section 'B' Upton. One map covers both sections; there is no suggested walk, as the locations are not numerous, and they are thinly spread over quite a large area.

Sidcup is divided into two sections - Section 'A' Central Sidcup; and Section 'B' Lamorbey & Blackfen. The introduction is extended to cover the areas of Footscray & North Cray, which are sometimes considered part of Sidcup. There are two maps, one for each section. There are suggested walks covering most locations in Section

7

'A' and all locations in the Lamorbey area of Section 'B'; Blackfen is not included, as the locations are not numerous and it is difficult to put together an interesting walk.

Footscray and North Cray, which are both included in the Sidcup introduction, are not divided into sections. There is a map for each area. There is a suggested walk covering most locations in Footscray, but no walk for North Cray as the locations (except for a cluster near Loring Hall) cover quite a large area, and crossing North Cray Road can be difficult.

Although the introductions to the areas contain some historical background, and certain locations have some historical information in indented paragraphs, the guide is not a history of Bexley and Sidcup; it makes no pretensions to be a work of local history or an antiquarian work. Again, although some non-specialist knowledge of architecture is assumed, the guide does not become involved in detailed architectural analysis and a conscious attempt has been made to avoid architectural jargon. Readers interested in further information on local history and architectural detail may like to consult the list of books at the end of the guide.

The gazetteers are intended as a comprehensive list of buildings and landscape features which are of visual interest, though the choice of places is inevitably very personal. The emphasis is on what is there now, not so much on what has been there in the past, and practical information is given on how best to see each place.

The maps, which are the key to the guide, adopt the same practical approach. Virtually every place mentioned in the text is pinpointed on a map in such a way as to make it easy to find and notice. The maps are indicative and not to scale, and only show those roads which are likely to be important to the visitor. It is suggested that a more detailed road map of the area also be obtained.

The starring system in the gazetteers enables visitors to allocate their time to the best advantage. All locations which are starred are, in my opinion, worth a very special effort to see. The stars are from one to three - three stars are given to locations which are of national importance; two stars to locations which are important in a London context; and one star to locations of particular local interest. Most locations however are not starred, but they are still in my view worth seeing; such places invariably have interesting features and help to make the area distinct.

Italics are used for information on access, for other practical advice, for introductory notes before the walks, and also for cross-referencing. Paragraphs with information of a specifically historical nature are indented.

The sequence of locations in the gazetteers generally follows the order in the suggested walks, and locations not included in the walks are slotted into the sequence in a way which indicates how visits might most conveniently be made.

Some locations are difficult of access, and the guide gives practical information on how to overcome this difficulty. In some cases this may not always be possible, but it is certainly worth trying. In other cases, a certain initiative is demanded; for example, it is usually necessary to phone or call at the clergyman's residence to obtain access to church interiors. In my experience most clergymen are extremely helpful in facilitating this. And many places which are private will not in practice turn away the interested visitor asking permission to view. The text includes contact telephone numbers and/or addresses which may be found helpful in this context.

Of the publications which I have consulted, I wish to make particular mention of: the section on Bexley, which is by John Newman, in 'London 2: South', by Bridget Cherry and Nikolaus Pevsner, in the Penguin Buildings of England series; the Department of the Environment List of Buildings of Architectural & Historic Interest, which can be consulted at the National Monuments Record, Fortress House, 23 Savile Row, London W1; the survey of buildings carried out by the Bexley Civic Society in the 1970s and early 1980s; and a whole series of informative publications by Bexley Libraries and Museums. These and other publications which I have found useful are listed in the bibliography at the end.

I also wish to give very special thanks and acknowledgment to numerous local people who helped me in various ways. Len Reilly and Malcolm Barr-Hamilton at the Local Studies Centre at Hall Place dealt courteously and efficiently with my many requests for information, some of which involved much painstaking work; they also read the whole text and gave me much valuable advice. Dr John Mercer read my text on Sidcup and The Crays, and made many helpful comments. Michael Dunmow read the 'industrial archaeology' entries and drew my attention to items which I would otherwise have overlooked. Also very helpful were Jim Packer, particularly with information on pubs; and both Martyn Nichols and John Davison, of the Bexley Planning Department, who gave me a lot of important information on a number of buildings. Clergymen at all the churches were helpful in facilitating my visits, but I would wish to make particular mention of the vicars and ministers at Old Bexley Baptist Church, St James Blendon, and the Holy Redeemer Blackfen. Many thanks also to Jim Pope for invaluable advice and help with production and design.

The area covered by this guide, like any urban area, is subject to the process of change, and the situation with regard to the condition and function (or even the existence) of buildings, their accessibility etc can change quite rapidly. However, the information was checked before going to print, and if anyone is misled in any way, I can only offer my apologies.

Darrell Spurgeon,

Blackheath, September 1993

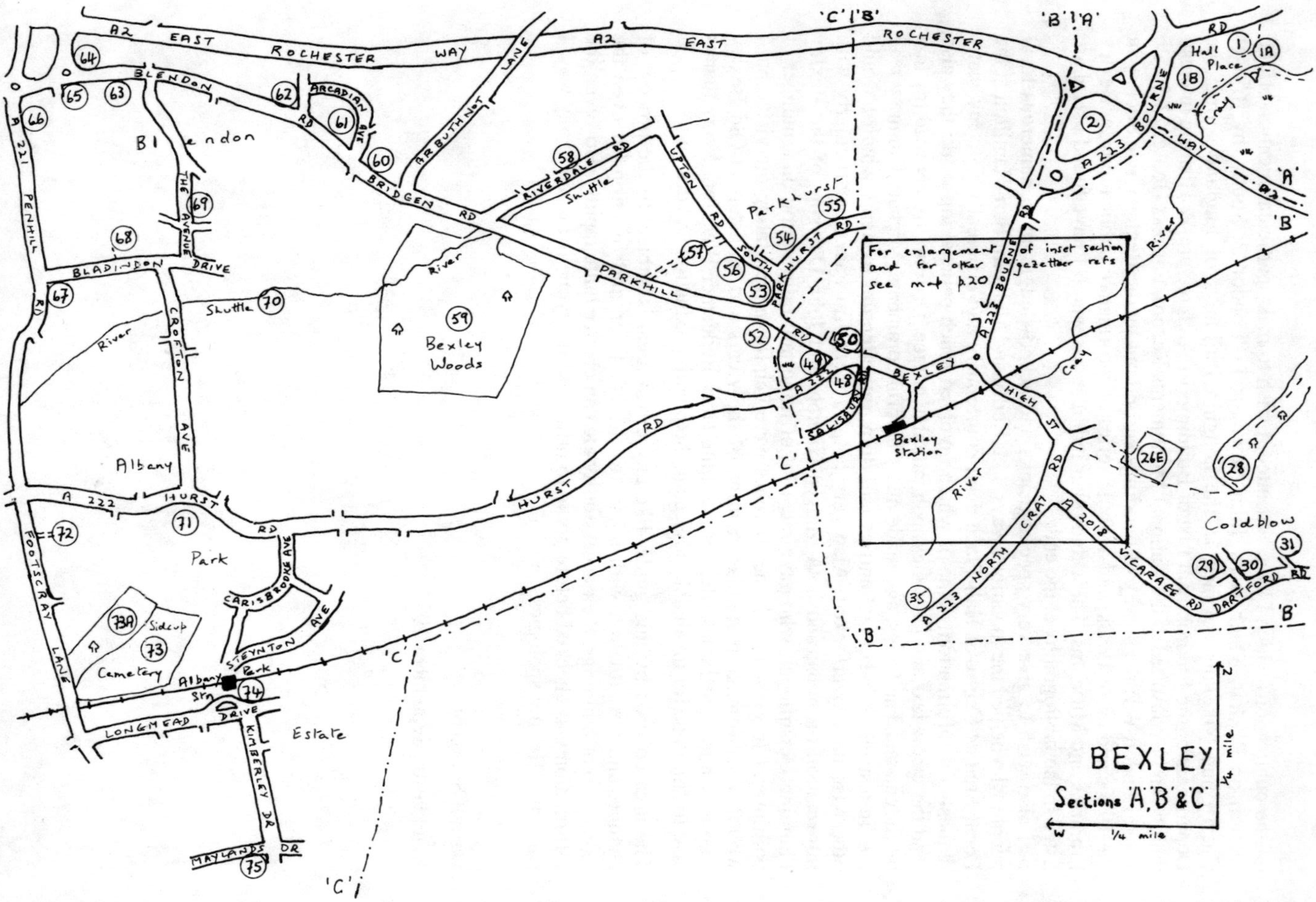
A2 EAST ROCHESTER WAY
A2 EAST ROCHESTER RD
'C' 'B'
'B' 'A'
Hall Place
Cray
BOURNE WAY
A 223
'A'
'B'
BLENDON
ARCADIAN AVE
RD
ARBUTHNOT LANE
Blendon
A 221 PENHILL RD
THE AVENUE
BLADINDON DRIVE
BRIDGEN RD
RIVERDALE RD
Shuttle
UPTON RD
Parkhurst
SOUTH PARKHURST RD
PARKHILL RD
River
Bexley Woods
Shuttle
CROFTON AVE
River
For enlargement of inset section and for other gazetteer refs see map p.20
A 223 BOURNE RD
BEXLEY
HIGH ST
Cray
River
Bexley Station
A 222
SALISBURY RD
HURST RD
'C'
Albany
A 222 HURST RD
Park
FOOTSCRAY LANE
CARISBROOKE AVE
STEYNTON AVE
Sidcup Cemetery
Albany Park Stn
LONGMEAD DRIVE
KIMBERLEY DR
MAYLANDS DR
Estate
'C'
'B'
River
A 2018 NORTH CRAY RD
A 223
VICARAGE RD
DARTFORD RD
Coldblow
'B'
BEXLEY
Sections 'A','B'&'C'
N
W
1/4 mile
1/4 mile
1
1A
18
2
28
26E
29
30
31
35
48
49
50
52
53
54
55
56
57
58
59
60
61
62
63
64
65
66
67
68
69
70
71
72
73
73A
74
75

# BEXLEY

## Introduction

The area of Bexley covered by the gazetteers which follow is shown on the maps on pages 10 & 32. In addition to Bexley Village and Hall Place, it also embraces the residential districts of Blendon, Albany Park and Parkhurst to the west, and Coldblow, Bexley Hospital and Joydens Wood to the east.
Bexley Village, one of the best preserved villages in London, is the focal point of the area. It has a medieval church, a genuine Tudor pub, many 18th century buildings, and some well-designed postwar buildings. Its High Street, still following its winding medieval line, has great charm and character.
It forms too a great traffic junction - the ancient road from Eltham to Dartford (via Parkhill Road, the High Street and Vicarage Road) is crossed by the ancient road from Crayford to Orpington (via Bourne Road and North Cray Road) at a point where a bridge crosses the River Cray, and the great railway viaduct of 1866 towers above.

### Early history

Substantial finds in 1957 near a modern housing estate at Cold Blow Crescent, to the east of Bexley Village, provide evidence of an Iron Age settlement just before the Roman Conquest.
Bexley Village itself almost certainly originated during the Saxon period. The Faesten Dyke, a linear earthwork in Joydens Wood, may have been created in the 5th century.
The old parish church of Bexley retains the outline of a Norman arch, and its present ground plan was largely established by the early 13th century. Around that period there was a manor house, which administered the affairs of the medieval manor of Bexley, on the site of the present house. There were many medieval buildings along the line of the present High Street as far west as Station Approach; and there were substantial medieval mansions nearby at Hall Place, Blendon and Baldwyns.

### Hall Place

The largest mansion in the area is Hall Place, on the River Cray to the north of the village. There was a house on or near this site at least by the 14th century, and there may have been a mill by the river here at that time.
The Tudor part of the present house was built c1540 for the merchant Sir John Champneis, and about a century later the merchant Sir Robert Austen added the red brick part to the south. The building with its two halves in totally contrasting styles forms an outstanding architectural ensemble.

The headquarters of Bexley Libraries and Museums is now located in the 17th century part, whilst Bexley Museum and the Local Studies Centre occupy rooms in the Tudor part.

## Bexley Village

The present High Street was largely built up by 1800, except for the section on the south side to the west of Station Approach. By 1850 North Cray Road had houses on its west side, whilst Bourne Road had a baptist chapel and a brewery, and further north, a school.

After the arrival of the railway and its viaduct in 1866 came the development of the rest of the High Street, and extended development southwards along North Cray Road and northwards along Bourne Road and Albert Road.

The railway also brought rapid development to the west of the Village, in the area of Parkhurst, and later in Salisbury Road.

## Parkhurst

The development of Parkhurst took place between 1869 and 1881, and consisted essentially of two planned projects in the grounds of two old houses - Marl House and Parkhurst House. A number of houses with extraordinary decorative features have survived from these projects.

The former grounds of Marl House were developed in 1869, on the west side of Upton Road South (no 232 was recently demolished, otherwise these houses have survived), and along the north side of Parkhill Road (only no 72 has survived, though greatly altered and extended).

The Parkhurst Estate was developed from 1876 on the former grounds of Parkhurst House, and has remained to a considerable extent unaltered. It embraces the area between Upton Road South and Parkhurst Road.

St Johns Church was built in 1882 to cater for this growing population, initially as a chapel-of-ease to St Marys. It became a parish church in its own right in 1936, by which time areas further west had been developed.

## Blendon & Bridgen

Further west were farmlands and the grounds of two 18th century mansions. Bridgen Place, east of Arbuthnot Lane, was demolished for housing development in the early 1920s. Blendon Hall, at the centre of a larger and very ancient estate south of Blendon Road, was demolished for housing in 1934.

East of Blendon is Bexley Woods; though reduced in size by housing development since 1900, it is still an extensive and delightful oasis. The River Shuttle runs across the north-west corner.

## The Shuttle Riverway

This signposted walkway follows the River Shuttle for much of its length of about five miles, and it is at its best in Blendon and Bridgen. The river rises in Pippenhall Meadows in Eltham, and eventually joins the River Cray near Hall Place. It first passes through Avery Hill Park in Eltham, then passes through Blackfen, and enters the Blendon area at the Penhill Bridge. It is possible to walk alongside the river right across Blendon, and much of the walk is quite delightful.

## Albany Park

To the south of Blendon is the large Albany Park Estate, built in the 1930s with its own sponsored railway station by New Ideal Homesteads *(see gazetteer no 74);* since the war an unusual church has been erected here.

The area also incorporates Hurst Place, an 18th century mansion, much altered and now in use as a community centre; Rutland Shaw, a small area of woodland; and Sidcup Cemetery.

## The old road to Dartford

To the east of Bexley Village, the scene becomes more rural, with fields and woods, and only scattered pockets of development.

North of Dartford Road is the housing area of Coldblow, perched on an escarpment above Churchfield Wood and looking back towards Bexley Village. A few houses were built at the end of the 19th century, and from this time two large houses have survived; but further development did not come until the 1930s and the postwar period.

Looming above to the south is the vast expanse of Joydens Wood, managed by The Woodland Trust. It is the largest area of woodland in the south-eastern suburbs of London.

Further on, the road called Baldwyns Park, developed for housing in the 1920s, leads south to the postwar housing development known as Joydens Wood, located to the east of the woodland and to the south of Bexley Hospital.

The great complex of Bexley Hospital, built from 1898 in the grounds of the ancient estate of Baldwyns, fronts the main road. Across the road is the small housing area of Maypole, built to accommodate the staff of the Hospital. Beyond is a large roundabout over the A2, and then one comes to Dartford Heath.

# BEXLEY

## Gazetteer

### Section 'A' HALL PLACE

**1. \*\*\*Hall Place.** This highly attractive and interesting building, with its wonderful location on the north bank of the River Cray, is made up of two parts in totally different architectural styles, but forming an outstanding architectural ensemble.

The northern part is of stone, basically c1540 with additions and alterations c1560, and consists of a central Great Hall with two long wings, each of two storeys, stretching northwards to Bourne Road. The stonework is mainly rubble with flint infill, though sections (around the Great Hall, and the tower on the west range) have a delightful chequerwork pattern; the chequerwork was originally intended to be extended to other areas of the building.

The southern part is of red brick, built 1649-c1660; it is also of two storeys, and is roughly square around a central courtyard. Long corridors on both storeys, linked by a grand staircase, serve to join the two parts of the building.

> There was a house on or near the site at least by the 14th century, occupied by the At-Hall family of Bexley. There may have been a mill by the river here at that time; the last mill on the site, a corn-mill, was demolished in 1926.
> The stone part of the present house was originally built c1540 for the merchant Sir John Champneis, whose memorial can be seen in St Marys Church, Bexley. The main entrance porch with a staircase was to the south, and there were another staircase in the tower at the western end. The additions and alterations c1560 gave the Tudor house its present more regular form.
> In 1649 it was sold to the merchant Sir Robert Austen, who by c1660 had added the red brick part to the south. The porch to the south was removed, and replaced by a tower containing a new staircase; the two parts were linked by corridors.
> Between 1772 and 1926 it was in the ownership of Sir Francis Dashwood (of Hellfire Club fame) and his family, though they rarely lived there.
> From 1917 the tenant was the Countess of Limerick, who made extensive internal alterations and introduced topiary into the gardens; she stayed there until her death in 1943. The house had been bought by Bexley Urban District Council in 1935, and in 1968 the London Borough of Bexley undertook extensive restoration, and rebuilt parts as replicas of the original.
> It then became the headquarters of Bexley Libraries and Museums, incorporating Bexley Museum and the Local Studies Centre.

The best view of the north, Tudor range is through the magnificent early 18th century wrought iron \*gates on Bourne Road. At the end of an enclosed garden is the Great Hall, with a pair of full-height bay windows on either side of a central doorway (which, though in Tudor style, is in fact modern). The two wings projecting forward were to the left the kitchen and service wing; and to the right the solar wing, including the chapel which projects slightly into the garden. The additions of c1560 included the left-hand central bay window, most of the right wing (beyond the chapel projection), and the end part of the left wing. The turret and cupola visible on top belong to the main staircase which is in the 17th century building behind.

Red brick walls, mainly late 17th century though incorporating some older stone sections and much restored, extend from the gates to the two wings of the building and stretch away on either side along the north side of the grounds.

The east, south and west ranges can be seen from the garden surrounding the building, which is entered through a gateway from the car park to the east.

By the entrance to the car park is **The Lodge**, c1872, with its great chimneystacks; alongside are old gates, also c1872, flanked by distinctive round pillars.

To the south of the car park are a Plant Nursery *(open to the public)*, with a greenhouse containing a wide variety of pot plants and a huge banana plant overhanging a pond, and The Jacobean Barn *(see below, page 17)*.

The east range consists of roughly equal sections of the 16th century stone building and the adjoining 17th century red brick building. The present main entrance to the building is near the centre of the range, and is actually in the 17th century part, though the doorway and the round-headed windows on either side are Tudor and have been repositioned here.

In the stone part, note the Tudor windows of different sizes, and the four projecting sections. The projection with the tiny windows at the upper level was the Tudor garderobe (or toilet).

As on the other ranges, the red brick part has a harmonious pattern of closely positioned windows; on the ground floor the windows are the original casements, set under recessed round arches. Note also the pedimented dormers, and the letter 'D' (for Dashwood) on top of a rainwater head; both these features occur more frequently on the other ranges.

The south range has a wide central pedimented wooden doorway. The row of pedimented dormers is particularly fine on this range.

On the west range, the stone part includes a tower and windows which were rebuilt in 1968 as replicas of the Tudor structure. The tower, which originally enclosed a spiral staircase, has very appealing chequerwork. To the north of the tower, the full-height bay was for the parlour (now the Local Studies Centre) below and for the main bedroom above. The smaller window beyond was for the Chapel; the section beyond this was added c1560. In the red brick part, note the two pairs of oval windows.

The **\*\*interior** is also of outstanding interest, though the public does not have access to all areas. However, those parts of greatest interest - the Great Hall and its gallery, the old main bedroom, the room which is now Bexley Museum, and the old parlour (now the Local Studies Centre), all forming part of the Tudor building - are open to the public. Apart from the Grand Staircase, the 17th century building is used as offices by Bexley Libraries, and there is no general public access.

*The public areas are open Mondays to Saturdays 1000-1700 (dusk in winter), and (in the summer only) Sundays 1400-1800; admission free. (The Great Hall is often in use for exhibitions, and on some such occasions it may be difficult to see the room properly.) Those with a special interest in viewing the areas normally closed to the public should ask at the Local Studies Centre, and it may be possible to arrange this.*

The main entrance on the east front leads into a long corridor extending the full width of the building. The half-timbered walls and ceiling were added by Lady Limerick in the 1920s. The 16th century part, with the Great Hall, is to the right, and the 17th century part, with the Grand Staircase, to the left.

The **Great Hall** is entered through a doorway on the right. It has a fine Tudor coved ceiling, with a total of 168 wooden bosses. The west bay window is of stone, c1540, and the east bay window of wood, c1560. Before this later addition, the gallery extended further into the hall, and had to be shortened before the second bay window could be built; above the entrance can be seen two adjacent doorways, which were earlier entrances to the gallery. In the south wall is a Tudor stone fireplace, with leaves in the spandrels. The panelling is 19th century. At the east end is an alcove, where a Tudor spiral staircase was located. At the west end is a magnificent organ dating from 1766, which is still in good working order and is occasionally played; it was brought here from Danson Mansion *(see Welling 9)* in 1974. From the hall windows one can see to the left the Gothic-style window of the original Chapel.

In the ground floor corridor are display-cases at present containing some of the finds of archaeological excavations in 1989 of a Roman site, which included well-pits and a small cremation cemetery, immediately to the west of the Guy Earl of Warwick pub, Park View Road, Welling. The finds, dating from the first to the fourth century AD, include part of a face-pot; fragments of a rotary quern used for grinding corn; and an indented beaker.

At the far end of the corridor a doorway leads into the original **Parlour**, now the **Local Studies Centre** *(open Mondays to Saturdays 0900-1700, dusk in winter)*. It has a largely 16th century ceiling (though the pillars are of 1960), an imported 17th century fireplace, and fine 19th century panelling. The inside offices include the original chapel; ask for permission to view the Gothic-style window from inside, and the old oak wainscotting, probably the only original panelling in the building.

The **grand staircase** is the original wooden staircase of 1653, though restored. It has great bulbous finials, pendants and balusters, and is in a large open well. Note the two oval windows and the circular window above; the other windows follow the flights of steps. The staircase is encased in a great tower, which was largely rebuilt in 1968 as a replica of the original; however, it cannot be seen fully from any public area, though the turret and cupola on top can be seen from outside.

The upper floor corridor also extends the full width of the building, and as in the ground floor corridor, the half-timbering was added by Lady Limerick. The panelling is 19th century.

The bust which can be seen at the top of the staircase above the upper floor is of the local sculptor John Ravera, and was sculpted by Joan Palmer.

Opposite the head of the staircase on the upper floor are three openings quite close together. The first two remain from the room above the Tudor entrance porch; to the left is the original doorway of c1540 into the extended gallery, and to the right a doorway constructed c1560 and originally linked to the shortened gallery by a short bridge. The third opening was constructed c1650 to lead directly into the shortened gallery and is still used for this purpose. To the right of this doorway is a transparent panel covering part of the exterior wall of the Tudor building; to the left of the doorway can be seen a small piece of moulded stonework from an earlier building which was used in the Tudor wall.

The gallery was remodelled in the 1920s by Lady Limerick. There are several exhibits; they include a deep Victorian spray bath of 1880 - the woodwork encases a water tank which could provide by means of spray jets a hot or cold shower, a douche or a plunge bath.

From the windows in the staircase and the upper corridor can be seen the central brick courtyard of the 17th century building. It was originally an open cloister, but the arcades were later bricked up and round-headed windows introduced, probably in the 19th century.

At the end of the corridor a doorway leads into the **main bedroom** of the Tudor house. This room was transformed c1660-80 by the addition of a quite fantastic early 17th century Jacobean ceiling, intricately and extravagantly ornamented with nudes, half-human half-plant figures, grotesque faces, animals, cherubs, curlicues, arabesques etc. The Jacobean fireplace of 1610, which is also ornate though rather more classical, was imported by Lady Limerick in the 1930s. This room is used by the Museum for special exhibitions.

The room leads into a smaller room, originally a picture gallery (hence the staggered arrangement of the windows) of c1560. It has a fine barrel-vaulted plaster ceiling added in the 18th century, ornate but restrained. This room now houses the permanent exhibition of *Bexley Museum, with important archaeological finds, as well as geological and wildlife exhibits.

The permanent exhibits include Stone Age axes; a second century Roman amphora and glass jar, with two bone cylinders and two brooches in the shape of stylised horses which were in the jar, found at Iris Avenue Bexleyheath 1973; pottery from a Romano-British village site excavated at Joydens Wood 1951; and stonework, pottery fragments, tiles, and medieval keys from Lesnes Abbey.

If access is gained to the areas normally closed to the public *(see above, page 15)*, it is most interesting to go into the courtyard for the view of the exterior of the tower enclosing the grand staircase. The courtyard is accessed through a large archway to the south; from here can also be seen how the arcades of the open cloister were enclosed, probably in the 19th century, by bricking up the other archways and introducing round-headed windows.

In the west range of the 17th century building is another original staircase, with bulbous finials and balusters. In the room beyond the staircase on the ground floor, now used as a mess-room, is a Tudor-style fireplace (probably imported) and a wooden spit rack of 1651. Other rooms contain 18th century shutters, 19th century panelling, and imported fireplaces.

There are several outbuildings to the east of the main building which are of great interest, particularly the Barn and the Stables.

**\*The Jacobean Barn (1A).** This pub / restaurant, opened 1990, consists of a magnificent late 17th century barn, used as the restaurant, and the Mill House, which is Edwardian at the front and probably late 18th century at the rear, used as the bar; they are linked together by a modern section. The barn has tremendous sloping roofs, and rows of tiny windows at the top of the gables at both ends; it was a threshing barn, with the old entrances still surviving opposite each other (to allow a cross draught). The interior has been well restored, using some original wooden roof beams.

In the courtyard behind is the **\*Stable Block**, also late 17th century, though the first floor was altered in the 19th century. This building is used in the summer months as a Visitors Centre, with an exhibition including farm machinery and implements, an old farm waggon, and reconstructions of a cooper's workshop, a blacksmith's forge, and a Victorian cottage kitchen.

The gate to the Stables is normally closed outside the summer months; if so, follow a lane to the left of the Barn. This gives access to the area of the Stables and the rear of the Mill House, and continues to the site of the old mill, which was demolished in 1926. There is an iron bridge over the river at this point, and the old sluice and weir can be seen.

Between the Barn and the main building is a **\*Granary**, brought here from Manor Farm, Bexley *(see 26D)*, in 1988. It is early 19th century, and is raised on 12 reconstructed staddlestones (which were designed to protect the grain from damp and vermin). The interior *(apply at the Local Studies Centre for access)* is divided by low wooden partitions into five bins or boxes where the grain was stored.

The **\*formal gardens (1B)** of Hall Place, going down to the River Cray and then south to the A2, are quite magnificent. They form part of an enormous area of open space, which extends to the north across Bourne Road to include an area of grassed parkland on a sloping site; and to the east to include playing fields north of the river, and grassland south to the railway line.

The formal gardens are to the west of the house; they were laid out from 1952 onwards. First one comes to the rose garden, and to the north, some fine examples of topiary, including the ten heraldic figures of the Queen's Beasts - they are, from east to west, the White Horse of Hanover, the Unicorn of Scotland, the Red Dragon of Wales, the Greyhound of Richmond, the Yale (a mythical beast with swivelling antlers) of Beaufort, the White Lion of Mortimer, the Black Bull of Clarence, the Falcon of the Plantagenets, the Griffin, and the Lion of England.

Behind the topiary are herbaceous borders along the north wall, and at the north-east corner, an old millstone set in the pathway. On the east wall nearer the house is a fountain head in the form of a demonic face, introduced by Lady Limerick.

Further west are the enclosed garden, the herb garden, and the sunken garden. Beyond is a bridge over the river to the south bank.

The walk along the south bank of the River Cray opposite Hall Place is particularly attractive, passing by a sluice and a weir at the site of the old mill; wagtails can frequently be seen at this point darting about the riverbank. At the end one comes to a beech hedge, beyond which to the left is a bridge leading to playing fields which extend to Bourne Road, and to the right a large area of grassland.

To the south are extensive rock and heather gardens, with a sunken pool. Beyond is a ditch, on the other side of which is a green space which has a particularly fine display of daffodils in the spring.

The ditch, which is often rather stagnant, was dug for flood prevention purposes in the 1960s, and is linked to the River Cray by a sluice at a point near the A2. On the other side of the A2 here the River Cray is joined by the River Shuttle.

**2. The Black Prince,** a rather splendid roadhouse type pub of 1933, with a picturesque frontispiece, half-timbered gables, and castellated chimneys. Its appearance is not enhanced by the **Forte Post House**, built alongside c1980.

# BEXLEY

## Gazetteer

### Section 'B' BEXLEY VILLAGE

*NB. For gazetteer numbers 1-2, 26E, 28-31, 35, and 48-50, see map on page 10; for gazetteer numbers 3-27, 32-34, 36-47, and 51, see map on page 20.*

3. *Bexley Station, Station Approach. Opened in 1866, this is the best preserved station on the Dartford Loop Line. The weatherboarded building on the down side, and the smaller building on the up side are basically original station buildings. The platform canopies are largely original too.
  At the bottom of Station Approach is a **K6 type of red cast-iron telephone kiosk**, designed by Sir Giles Gilbert Scott in 1935. (There are no surviving examples in the Bexley area of the K2 type of kiosk, designed by Scott in 1927. The K2 type has all panes of glass of the same size, whereas the K6 type features narrow rectangular panes of glass.)

4. *Stylemans Almshouses, 13/35 Bexley High Street. A symmetrical terrace of 12 houses of 1755, low-lying and austere. They are most attractive, with pleasing brickwork. The windows above the doors were inserted in 1961; they could be considered to have made the facade seem rather unbalanced.
  Under the central pediment is a plaque inscribed 'Stylemans Almshouses erected in the year 1755', and below a sundial inscribed '1882 tempus fugit'. The almshouses were erected under a trust set up by John Styleman, who lived at Danson, Welling, from 1695 to 1723.

5. *57 Bexley High Street, called Jackson House. A fine brick house, probably of 1676, set back from the road, with a projecting two-storey porch. The long extension to the rear, weatherboarded to the west, is later; the dormers were added in the early 19th century. (The date 1676 can be seen scratched on a brick near the left corner.)

6. St John Fisher Church, Thanet Road. A Roman Catholic church of 1974, with a strikingly wide open porch, like a porte-cochere. A tiny fleche sticks out of the large, sweeping pyramidal roof.
  The interior *(contact the presbytery next door at 48 Thanet Road, or ring 0322 524813)* has a square plan, and is lit by a narrow clerestory midway down the roof.

7. Freemantle Hall, 63 Bexley High Street. A building of 1894, looking rather incongruous in this location. It has a small clock tower (added in 1920) at the junction of three gables (one tile-hung, one brick, and one half-timbered). It was built and is still in use as a public hall.

19

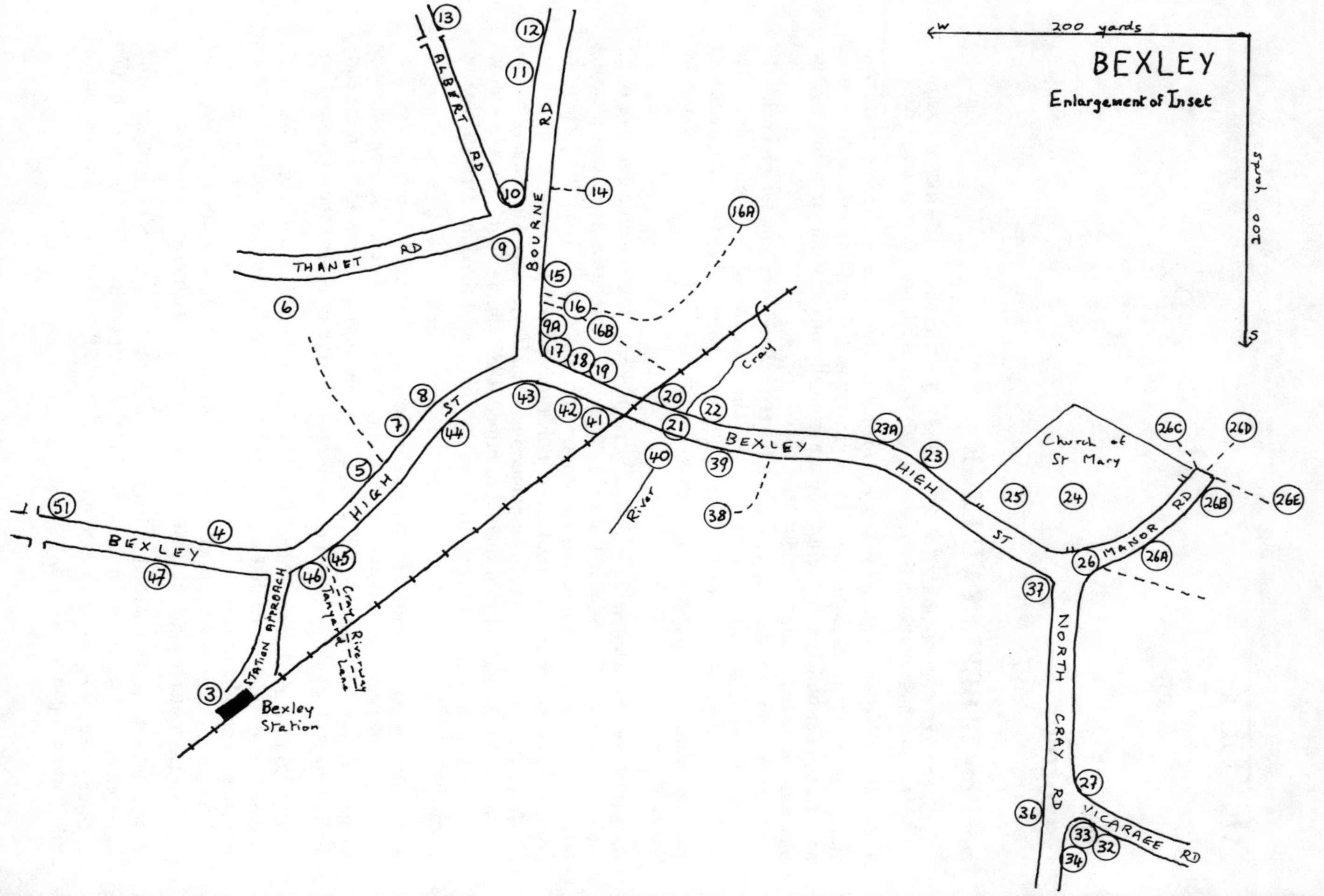

BEXLEY
Enlargement of Inset
W
200 yards
S
200 yards
BOURNE RD
ALBERT RD
THANET RD
HIGH ST
BEXLEY HIGH ST
BEXLEY
STATION APPROACH
Bexley Station
Cray Riverway
Tanyard Lane
River
Cray
Church of St Mary
MANOR RD
NORTH CRAY RD
VICARAGE RD
3
4
5
6
7
8
9
9A
10
11
12
13
14
15
16
16A
16B
17
18
19
20
21
22
23
23A
24
25
26
26A
26B
26C
26D
26E
27
32
33
34
36
37
38
39
40
41
42
43
44
45
46
47
51

8. *The Kings Head, 65 Bexley High Street. A fine timber-framed pub, basically late 16th century. The main part parallel with the road, including the gable to the right, is largely the original building. The late 19th century extension in front is unfortunate; there are rear extensions too.

Adjacent are **67/71 Bexley High Street**, a group of three cottages of the early 19th century, with modern shopfronts.

9. **Old Bexley Baptist Chapel**, Bourne Road. A building of 1905, consisting of the Sunday school to the left and the chapel to the right, forming an imposing architectural ensemble. Note the variety of window shapes and the amazing skyline of gables.

The **interior** is worth viewing *(contact the Pastor, 1a St Thomas Court, 0322 521785)*, as so much of the original wooden furniture has been preserved, including the pews, the pulpit and rostrum, and the hammerbeam roof.

Nearly opposite are **1/3 Bourne Road (9A)**, a pair of shops converted from the original Strict Baptist Chapel of 1846 after it moved across the road in 1905. The main shape of the chapel (which was oriented to the north) remains, but the frontage was of course changed and the north windows removed.

10. **Bexley Village Library**, 12 Bourne Road, a tiny but intriguing building of 1912 by Sir Edward Maufe, with some nice tilework. The original entrance was to the south, as can readily be detected.

11. **Victoria Homes**, 54/64 Bourne Road. These almshouses of 1897 consist of a pedimented central building flanked by two wings. Note the terracotta cresting right along the roofline.

12. **66/70 Bourne Road**, the former **Bexley National School**, has two separate buildings fronting the road. The whole complex has since 1974 been in industrial use.

The imposing building to the right has two shaped gables, each bearing a tablet, making up the words 'Built 1834'. It was the teacher's house; adjoining behind are the two original schoolrooms, also of 1834.

To the left is the old school-hall c1900, sympathetic in style with a similar shaped gable.

13. **The Black Horse**, Albert Road. This pleasing pub of the 1850s is the focal point of a mid 19th century enclave around the northern part of Albert Road, the area at that time being called Building Fields.

14. **17/19 Bourne Road** are of the 1860s; they flank the driveway to the former buildings of **Reffells Brewery**, where brewing took place from 1874 to 1956. No 17 (with a bow window) was used as the shop, and alongside is an old storehouse. No 19 (with a pediment) was used as offices. Note the water-tower behind. The premises now form Old Bexley Business Park.

**15. 11 Bourne Road** is a strange building of 1890 set back from the road. The upper floor has a strange gable, and there are urns on the projecting ground floor. It was originally called Ypsilanti, occupied by one of the Reffell brothers who owned the Brewery; it was subsequently a post office.

In front are two **K6 telephone kiosks**, designed by Sir Giles Gilbert Scott in 1935 *(see also 3)*.

**16. 5 Bourne Road.** Here are two adjacent driveways. The driveway to the left leads to the chemicals factory of Pharmax. The building right at the end of the site, with its series of round-headed windows, was the old **electricity generating station (16A)** built c1903 for Bexley Council Tramways.

The driveway to the right leads to Bourne Works; the arches under the railway viaduct at the end of the site are now in industrial use. Before 1866 there was a brewery, known as **Kent Brewery**, on the site, and the terrace of cottage-like buildings to the left were used as **stables and malthouses (16B)**. The brewery house is now 85 Bexley High Street *(see 19)*; other brewery buildings were demolished for the railway.

**17.** Note on the upper floor of 77a Bexley High Street (a building c1912) the old iron **finger signboards** pointing to 'Dartford' and 'The Crays'.

**18. The Millers Arms**, 81 Bexley High Street., a rather jolly pub of 1900.

**19. 85 Bexley High Street**, a building of late 18th century origin, though much altered (with a late 19th century shopfront), which was (probably from 1844) the brewery house for the Kent Brewery *(see 16B)*.

**20. Thomas Shearley Court,** 95 Bexley High Street. The tower hard by the railway viaduct is the dominant feature (and a bold architectural flourish) of this attractive building c1990, located between the railway and the river. Note also the timber oriels which merge up into the dormers in the striking roof. It is a housing development, stretching quite a way back alongside the river.

**21. Bexley Bridge**, over the River Cray. The present bridge was built in 1872. The first road bridge was probably constructed in the late 18th century.

**22. 101 Bexley High Street,** a fine small mid 18th century house, with a projecting pedimented central bay.

Adjacent are **nos 107/115,** a terrace of early 19th century cottages, greatly altered, made up of two groups under two separate roofs. The right-hand group, nos 111/5, may conceal some early 17th century structure.

**23. *Highstreet House,** 123 Bexley High Street. A highly attractive brick Georgian house, built in 1761. It was in fact a rebuild and enlargement of a much earlier (probably Tudor) house, the roof of which is visible to the rear when the house is looked at from the side. The two sloping sections on either side are also of 1761, but the long one-storey extension on the right is late 19th century. A blue plaque on the front states: 'John Thorpe, historian and antiquary, lived here c1750-1789'.

The fine ornamental front doorcase has a pediment and two engaged Ionic columns. A more simple Georgian pedimented doorcase to the garden front is visible from the adjacent churchyard.

The wall separating the house from the churchyard is Tudor in part. Just over the wall is a tablet to John Thorpe's wife, Catharina Thorpe, who died in 1789 *(see 25)*.

Note also the fire-engine shed, with its pantiled roof, at the front corner adjoining the churchyard; it is probably of 1761. The iron front railings are partly original.

To the west is **Brook Cottage (23A),** 117 Bexley High Street. The central projecting part and the section to the left were originally the coach-house and stables for Highstreet House, c1860-70, though much altered. The extension to the right is of the 1970s. Note in the wall to the left sections of the original Tudor boundary wall for the house which preceded Highstreet House.

**24. \*\*Church of St Mary.** A medieval church with a unique two-stage spire; it was the original parish church of Bexley. Though substantially restored by Basil Champneys in 1883, its medieval form has largely survived, and it is of outstanding interest.

The church consists of a nave and chancel, extended by the sanctuary at one end and the tower at the other, and a wide north aisle which extends into a chapel.

> There was a church on the site at the time of the Domesday Survey 1086. It was rebuilt in the late 12th century, taking the form of the present tower base, nave and chancel. The north aisle was added and the chancel extended to form the present sanctuary in the early 13th century, and the spire was probably added at that time. The north aisle chapel was added in the 14th century, thus completing the ground plan of the present church.
>
> In 1883 a substantial restoration was carried out by Basil Champneys. This included refacing the exterior in flint, rebuilding the east and north walls of the chancel, new east windows in the chancel and the north aisle, restoration of all other windows, new porches to south and north, and completely new internal woodwork. In 1956 the roof was re-tiled and the ceiling removed, with the medieval timberwork restored and left open to view.

The most striking external feature is the unusual two-stage shingled spire, probably early 13th century; the top stage is octagonal and the lower part tetragonal (with bell openings in the form of dormers), like a cone on top of a pyramid. (The spire is unique, though reminiscent of a few churches in Kent - Brookland on Romney Marsh, Willesborough near Ashford, and Upchurch near Gillingham.)

Only the two east windows were totally reconstructed in 1883. All the other windows remain basically medieval, though restored. There are eight lancet windows, all late 12th century except the one in the north aisle, which is 13th century. The two porches (which are in front of medieval doorways) and all the buttresses belong to the 1883 restoration.

Note, on cornerstones at the south-east corner of the nave, the remains of five small medieval scratch-dials, used either as sundials or to indicate the times of mass. Three are well preserved, and all have holes where pointers were fitted.

The **\*\*interior** is well worth viewing, particularly for the unusual Castilayn and Sparrow brasses, and for the Champeneis and other fine monuments. *(Contact the Vicarage, 29 Hill Crescent, 0322 523457, or 72 Rochester Drive, 0322 551741.)*

Inside the south porch, note the outline of a Norman arch with chevrons over the 13th century doorway.

The nave arcade is 13th century, and is continued by a wide 14th century arch, slightly skewed to the south, between the chancel and the north aisle chapel. The elaborate and intricately traceried chancel screen, with a rood loft above, and the screen between chancel and chapel were designed by Champneys 1883, as was the pulpit; note the strange conical cap of the turret alongside the chancel screen, reconstructed in 1883. The stained glass throughout is of 1883.

The interior is absolutely crammed with monuments. The more interesting monuments and other furnishings are mentioned in order, going clockwise from the south entrance.

Above the south entrance door is a tablet to Catharina Thorpe (wife of John Thorpe of Highstreet House) 1789, and alongside, a monument to Lady Mary Cosein 1683 with two putti holding up a cloth.

In the southwest corner of the nave is the font of 1684 (though the base is older), and on the floor, gravestones to members of the Styleman family. Above, on the west wall of the nave, is a fine cartouche to Anne Traveis 1679; and, to the left of the organ, a black tablet to Sir Richard Ford 1678. Against the wall is a pew of 1809, the only pre-1883 pew to survive.

In the north aisle, many of the pews (which are of 1883) have on the sides the names of three large mansions in the area - Hall Place, Blendon and Danson - for whose use they were originally reserved. On the easternmost arch of the arcade is an elegant tablet to Lady Isabel Dashwood 1858.

On the wall of the north aisle is a very classical monument to Edward Austen 1704; and further along, a classical tablet to Sir Edward Brett 1685. Under the easternmost window is a unique brass of a hunting horn, all that remains of a larger brass to Henry Castilayn 1407. At the very end of the north aisle wall is a monument to Sir John Champeneis 1590, with two small kneeling figures, nicely coloured and certainly the most interesting monument in the church.

On the east wall of the north aisle are two rectangular inscribed brasses to John Shelley 1441 and his wife, and a large and lively marble monument to Sir Robert Austen 1666, with twisted columns and other classical flourishes.

In the sanctuary, on the floor to the left of the altar is a charming brass of Thomas Sparrow 1513 wearing a long robe, and above it, close to the floor, a small inscribed brass to Margaret Bunton 1585. On the right wall of the sanctuary are the medieval piscina and three sedilia.

On the south wall of the nave is a large monument to John Styleman erected c1750.

**25. St Marys Churchyard.** At the western end of the pathway is an old lychgate, early 18th century, its roof supported on six oak posts. It was replaced in its original position at the south corner of the churchyard by a splendidly elaborate lychgate of 1891, with Gothic tracery, probably by Basil Champneys.

The churchyard contains numerous tombs and memorials. The oldest is the tomb-chest to the Payne family 1603, under the yew tree near the old lychgate.

On the old wall (which is Tudor in part) separating the churchyard from Highstreet House, note the tablet to Catharina Thorpe (wife of John Thorpe) 1789, with a large sandstone boulder underneath.

Nearby is a brick shed of 1844, which adjoins the older fire-engine shed in the garden of Highstreet House *(see 23)*.

**26. Manor Road.** Opposite the churchyard is **Manor Lodge (26A),** which used to be the lodge for the Manor House. The right-hand part, of brick and flint, is early 19th century, with later extensions to the left and rear.

After the church hall (which is of the 1980s) is **Manor Cottage (26B),** a large house c1870, and beyond this Manor Road ends with three driveways.

The one to the left leads to the ***Manor House (26C).** This important old house cannot be seen from the road, but there are views (though not very satisfactory) over the churchyard wall. The older part of the house is the southern part, probably early 18th century (though it may contain structure dating back to c1536), two storey, stuccoed, multi-gabled. The brick extension to the north was added c1800.

The driveway straight ahead leads to **Manor Farm (26D).** The main buildings here are modern, though with some earlier outbuildings. A granary on staddlestones was moved from here to the grounds of Hall Place *(see 1A)* in 1988.

The lane to the right leads to ***St Marys Cemetery (26E),** which was opened in 1857 as an overflow burial ground for St Marys Churchyard. It is rather overgrown, but has a special atmosphere, and is now maintained as a nature reserve by the London Wildlife Trust.

**27. 33 North Cray Road,** a pleasant house nicely rounding the corner with Vicarage Road; a foundation stone reads 'Bexley Workingmens Club 1898'.

**28. Churchfield Wood.** A long crescent of woodland, along a slope under the residential area of Coldblow and overlooking Manor Farm. A footpath, part of the Cray Riverway, runs along the bottom.

**29. 7 Hill Crescent.** A striking modernist house of the 1930s, with white walls, long horizontal bands of windows rounding the corners, and a glazed staircase head leading to a flat roof.

**30. Henleys,** 70 Dartford Road. A very large gaunt house, probably c1880, with Gothic doorcase and dormers. It is one of two houses surviving from the early development of Coldblow; the other is:

**31. Heathcroft,** 56 Dartford Road, a large house, probably c1880, similar to Henleys.

**32. 6/8 Vicarage Road,** a pair of early 19th century cottages, with later porches. Adjoining is **The Rising Sun,** a pub c1890, now closed.

**33. St Marys Home,** Vicarage Road. A rambling and irregular late 19th century building, formerly the vicarage, now a home for elderly persons.

The small building on the corner, **St Marys Cottage,** is a conversion of mid 19th century stables; the weatherboarded oriel is modern.

**34. Coach & Horses,** 35 North Cray Road. This pub is basically a mid 18th century building, though the weatherboarding on the frontage is a postwar addition. Note the two mounting blocks in front.

**35. 104 North Cray Road,** called The Cottage, a brick house of 1720.

**36. 30/34 North Cray Road.** An interesting group on the west side of the junction with Vicarage Road. It consists of:
**No 34**, called Heritage House, basically early 18th century, with a frontage refaced in stock brick in the mid 19th century.
**Nos 32 a/b**, which are of the early 1900s.
**No 32**, an early 19th century stuccoed house.
**Vale Lodge,** no 30, a house of 1824 with a prominent Doric porch.

**37. 16 North Cray Road / 106/8 Bexley High Street.** This varied group forms part of a terrace rounding the corner of North Cray Road with Bexley High Street. It is made up as follows:
**16 North Cray Road**, basically c1800, with a later bay window and left extension; it is becoming derelict.
**6/14 North Cray Road** are of 1821.
**4 North Cray Road** is mid 19th century Italianate.
**2 North Cray Road**, with a bargeboarded gable, rebuilt probably late 19th century.
**110/112 Bexley High Street** are mid 19th century, similar to 4 North Cray Road.
**106/8 Bexley High Street**, a fanciful house of 1888 with all sorts of unusual decorative detail and a coach entrance archway through the centre.

**38. Clarendon Mews**, an attractive housing development of the late 1980s, located behind and in the former grounds of Cray House. Note the enclosed garden square, the black timber oriel facing the approach drive, and the striking roof.

**39. *Cray House**, 96 Bexley High Street. A fine well-proportioned brick Georgian house, probably of 1775. There is a later extension to the left, and the small stuccoed bow on the right was added later too.

**40. *The Old Mill**, a pub / restaurant, opened 1972. It is a virtual replica of a weatherboarded corn-mill c1779, which had burned down in 1966. Note the projecting timber cabin, which was a lucarne, or hoist-house for lifting sacks to an opening below.
In the ground floor bar can be seen a wooden water-wheel (a modern innovation), and through a glass panel in the floor, the River Cray rushing along underneath.
**Mill Cottage**, alongside, is basically late 18th century, though much altered.
The location of The Old Mill behind Bexley Bridge is delightful, with a forecourt with willow trees overhanging the river. A pleasant section of the river can also be viewed from the car park behind.

**41. Mill Row**, a stylish development c1989 of six shops under the arches of the railway viaduct of 1866.

**42. 82/84 Bexley High Street**, an interesting pair, probably early 19th century, though considerably altered, with modern shopfronts.

**43. The George**, 74 Bexley High Street, a pleasing, largely stuccoed pub. It was there by 1717, but its present frontage is of the late 1870s. Interesting, bare interior.

**44. 48/68 Bexley High Street.** This shop terrace of 1966, following the slight curve in the road, is lively, with weatherboarded upper floors, and harmonious, despite the variety of shopfronts. There is a similar but smaller group of five shops, **nos 76/80**, further east.

**45. The Railway Tavern**, 38 Bexley High Street. The oldest part of this pub is to the left - a recessed upper floor c1700. The pub-front below and the part to the right are probably late 19th century.

**46. *34/36 Bexley High Street.** A fine brick pair of 1787, with later dormers and 19th century shopfronts. The building was until c1834 the parish workhouse. (On some of the bricks near the bottom of the upper floor windows can be seen, though with difficulty, the date 1787 and initials of parish vestry members.)

**47. Oxford Terrace**, 2/28 Bexley High Street. This terrace was built as a shopping parade in 1878, with the upper floors set back behind the line of the shopfronts. (No 14 has been rebuilt.)

**48. United Reformed Church.** A Victorian Gothic ragstone church of 1890 by George Baines. Note the miniature steeple alongside the north front, the dormer to the east, and the tiny bellcote. The interior is attractive, with a fine wooden roof *(contact 0322 522543).*

**49. War Memorial.** A large white cross of 1920, strategically located in front of a triangular green field, once called **Fair Field**. The field is a focal point for the area, and has fulfilled the function of a village green; it was the venue for the Bexley Fair in the 19th century.

**50. Park House.** The central and rear parts formed an early 19th century detached villa; the substantial gabled extension to the east, the smaller extension to the west, and the bargeboarded porch are all additions of the late 1890s.

**51. 1/3 & 7/9 Bexley High Street.** Two plain late 18th century pairs with brick front and weatherboarded rear; nos 1/3 have weatherboarded sides too.

# BEXLEY

## Gazetteer

### Section 'C' PARKHURST, BLENDON & ALBANY PARK

**52. *Church of St John the Evangelist**, Parkhill Road. A large, imposing Victorian Gothic ragstone church by George Low 1882. The tall and rather elegant spire, added to the tower in 1890, is quite a landmark; it now has a distinct inclination to the south. The church has a fine open location, particularly viewed across Fair Field.
> The church was built as a chapel-of-ease for the Parish Church of St Mary, Bexley Village, to cater for the growing population to the west which followed the arrival of the railway. It became a parish church in its own right in 1936.

The **interior** is worth viewing *(contact the Vicarage, 29 Parkhill Road, or telephone 0322 521786)* for the elaborately decorated chancel, with its canted apse. Behind an elegant iron screen the chancel has intricately stencilled walls and roof, and colourful stained glass windows. The lofty nave has clerestoried windows above arcades on both sides, and a large west window with stained glass of 1924.

**53. Island House**, 68 Parkhurst Road. A fine house of 1880, with a castellated bay window and pretty bargeboarding. It forms an island site with Parkhurst Gardens.

In front of the house, on Parkhill Road, is a rare example of a **Penfold hexagonal pillar box**, of the late 1870s.

**54. 50/64 Parkhurst Road.** This group includes some fanciful houses of the period 1878-81. Note in particular, from south to north:
**No 64,** of 1881, with Gothic door and windows.
**No 62,** of 1878, with a castellated bow window.
**No 60,** of 1881, with a great dentilled gable over a Gothic window.
**Nos 50/52,** of 1881, a large pair with a dentilled cornice over great bay windows.

**55. 32/42 Parkhurst Road.** A series of ornate detached villas of 1879-80 along a curve in the road. They have similar decorative features, including Gothic porches with elaborate plasterwork, Gothic upper floor windows, bay windows topped by balconies with open stonework featuring mythical animals, and polychrome brickwork.

**56. 234/240 Upton Road South.** This group is of 1869, and has some houses with extraordinary features. (The even more extraordinary no 232, the former University School, was recently demolished.) Two houses in particular stand out:
**No 240,** called Laurel House, with castellated parapet and bay window, and a tiny turret.

28

No 234, with its amazing elongated and bargeboarded frontispiece sticking up through the roofline.

**57. Cross Lane.** This narrow winding lane with its lines of tall trees has retained a rural character.

**58. Riverdale Road.** This section of the Shuttle Riverway is quite delightful, grassed on both sides, with the river gently winding and rippling over a series of shallow weirs.

**59. *Bexley Woods.** This tract of woods (mainly coppiced hornbeam trees) is surprisingly extensive. It has a special atmosphere, with the River Shuttle at the north-west corner, looking quite natural as it twists and turns, and the woods ascending gradually to the east.

**60. 1/11 Bridgen Road.** Two groups of cottages of the 1820s. Next is **no 13**, a small but tall detached house, dated 1827.

**61. Arcadian Avenue.** A crescent of mock-Tudor houses, mainly semi-detached, of the 1930s. The original design for the pairs (unfortunately altered in many cases) included a shared gabled and projecting frontispiece with half-timbering above an open porch, and ground floor oriel windows on either side. The pattern continues into Woodside Lane and into Blendon Road, but without the sense of enclosure which makes Arcadian Avenue itself quite delightful.

**62. 44 Blendon Road.** This irregular brick building with its odd little bellcote was formerly **Bridgen National School**, of 1860.

**63. *Jays Cottages**, 119/123 Blendon Road. This highly attractive group of three houses was originally a pair of cottages built c1700. The windows and bargeboarded side gables are later alterations; the extensions to the east and the rear are c1939.

**64. *Three Blackbirds**, Blendon Road. An attractive mid 18th century pub with a fine roof. Modern porch and extension to the west.

**65. West Lodge,** 167 Blendon Road. A jolly stone building c1860, with four Dutch gables, two of them rather fanciful. It was one of two lodges for Blendon Hall.

> The estate of Blendon, originally called Bladigdone, goes back at least to the 13th century. Early tenants included John and Maud de Bladigdone, whose brass is in the new East Wickham church *(see Welling 13)*, and Henry Castilayn, whose brass is in St Marys Church Bexley. The last mansion on the estate was Blendon Hall, built for Lady Mary Scott in 1763; Humphrey Repton later landscaped the grounds. The house was demolished in 1934, and the grounds have been developed for housing; a lodge, the bailiff's house, and many trees have survived.

**66. Blendon Methodist Church.** Alongside the red brick church of 1972 is the old white concrete church of 1935, a long low-lying building in art deco style, now in use as the hall. It was an avant-garde building for its time, and still looks more like a pavilion or cinema of that age than a former church.

**67. Church of St James the Great.** A low-lying red brick church of 1937, the parish church of Blendon. Note the open bell turret.

The interior is worth seeing *(contact the Vicarage, 37 Bladindon Drive, 081-301 5387)* for the rather charming chancel, with its series of narrow round-headed windows. Note on the right-hand wall a small stone V moulding which is actually Norman from Rochester Cathedral *(see also Sidcup 37)*.

**68. The Bailiffs House,** 23a Bladindon Drive (accessible along a lane between nos 23 & 25). This is a handsome house - the section to the right with bargeboarded porch and first floor windows was the original house built c1855 for the Blendon Estate; the gabled projecting extension to the left is postwar.

**69. The Avenue** has a footway down the centre flanked by an avenue of lime trees, which used to lead to Blendon Hall.

**70. Riverside Walk.** This is a pleasant walk, leading from Bexley Woods to Lamorbey Park; it is part of the Shuttle Riverway. Nearer the Park, around the Penhill Bridge (built 1917), is a colony of water voles, which can often be seen at quiet times of the day during the summer months.

**71. *Hurst Place,** Hurst Road. A fine stuccoed classical villa, now the Hurst Community Centre. The front part is basically c1770, though the cellars are reputed to be of 1720. Additions c1860 included the north porch, and the long rear extension with bows to the west and at the rear. It was bought by Bexley Borough Council in 1946 and became a community centre in 1955.

**72. Cottage Field Close** is an attractive enclave of terraced houses, reminiscent of Old Forge Way *(see Sidcup 7)* but built 1977-8. As at Old Forge Way, all the upper floors are tile-hung, weatherboarded or half-timbered, the ground floors red brick.

**73. Sidcup Cemetery,** Foots Cray Lane. This cemetery was opened in 1912. It has no landscape interest; but it has a fine location, with the railway in a deep cutting to the south, and **Rutland Shaw (73A),** a pleasant small area of woodland, to the north.

**74. Albany Park Station** was opened in 1935, being partly funded by New Ideal Homesteads, who were at that time building the Albany Park Estate in the area. The original brick building faces Steynton Avenue to the north, where there is a shopping centre and a mock-Tudor pub, The Albany; there is another entrance via a short lane from Longmead Drive to the south. Both entrances lead to a footbridge, from which stairs lead down to the platforms in a cutting. The original platform canopies have survived.

> New Ideal Homesteads were the most prolific housing developers in the London area in the 1930s. Founded in 1929 by Leo Meyer, who had been a surveyor for Erith UDC, it built large estates at relatively low prices. They were mainly semi-detached houses, mostly in the chalet style, though there were bungalows and terraces as well. The greatest concentration of their estates was in South East London, and particularly in the area between the Bexleyheath and the Sidcup railway lines. For two of their larger estates in the area, Albany Park and Falconwood Park, they sponsored the opening of new stations on the lines.

**75. Church of St Andrew,** Maylands Drive. An ingenious modern church of 1964, squat and octagonal; it is perched on top of the parish hall, on a sloping site. The entrance is through a glazed porch and along a glazed bridge. The copper roof with its four glazed gables slopes steeply upwards to a tall copper fleche.

The **interior** *(contact the Vicarage , St Andrews Road, phone 081-300 4712)* is quite striking; it is lit by the gables, and the roof sweeps up to a central point.

# BEXLEY

## Gazetteer

### Section 'D' BEXLEY HOSPITAL & JOYDENS WOOD

**76. Bexley Hospital.** A great complex of buildings, opened 1898 in the grounds of Baldwyns Park, which previously belonged to Baldwyns Mansion *(see 77)*. The mansion is along a road to the right from the entrance.

Other buildings of interest in the complex include the lodges on either side of the entrance gates; the great castellated water tower, which is a landmark for miles around; and along the road to the left, the neo-Georgian **chapel (76A)** of 1899. Much of the complex is no longer in use.

**77. *Baldwyns Mansion** is a stuccoed villa, probably c1802, with the entrance recessed between two giant Ionic columns; there is a full-height bow to the left. It is highly attractive, though it is becoming derelict.

> The mansion was occupied by the American inventor Sir Hiram Maxim in the 1890s, when he conducted his experiments in the construction of an early flying machine in the adjoining Park.

**78.** The area of **Maypole**, opposite the entrance gates, was developed to house staff at Bexley Hospital. Two long terraces interrupted by great gables, in Baldwyns Road and Denton Terrace (facing Dartford Heath), remain from the Edwardian period.

At the end of Baldwyns Road, a path to the left leads to **Broomhills (78A)**, a large late 19th century house in Tudor style, now derelict. The old lodge, also derelict, is on Old Bexley Lane.

**79.** At the north-east corner of the grounds of Bexley Hospital, outside 1 Dartford Road, is a **coal duty boundary marker,** a cast iron post carrying the City of London shield, and the inscription: 'Regents Canal Ironworks London, Henry Grissell 1861'.

> The surviving boundary markers, which are in several different shapes and sizes, demarcate the area round London covered by the London Coal & Wine Duties Continuance Act 1861. The Corporation of the City of London already had the right of charging for coal brought into the metropolitan area, and this right lasted till 1889.

**80. 107 Tile Kiln Lane,** formerly called Oak Cottage, an octagonal house c1840 with a thatched roof, with extensions of the 1960s to the rear. It was originally one of the lodges to Mount Mascal, and is similar to Avenue Lodge *(see North Cray 11)*.

**81. St Barnabas Church**, Tile Kiln Lane, was built as a church hall in 1971; it became a church after a small sanctuary had been added in 1980.

In the left-hand corner of the grounds is another **coal duty boundary marker** *(see 79)* bearing the City of London shield.

# BEXLEY
## Section 'D'

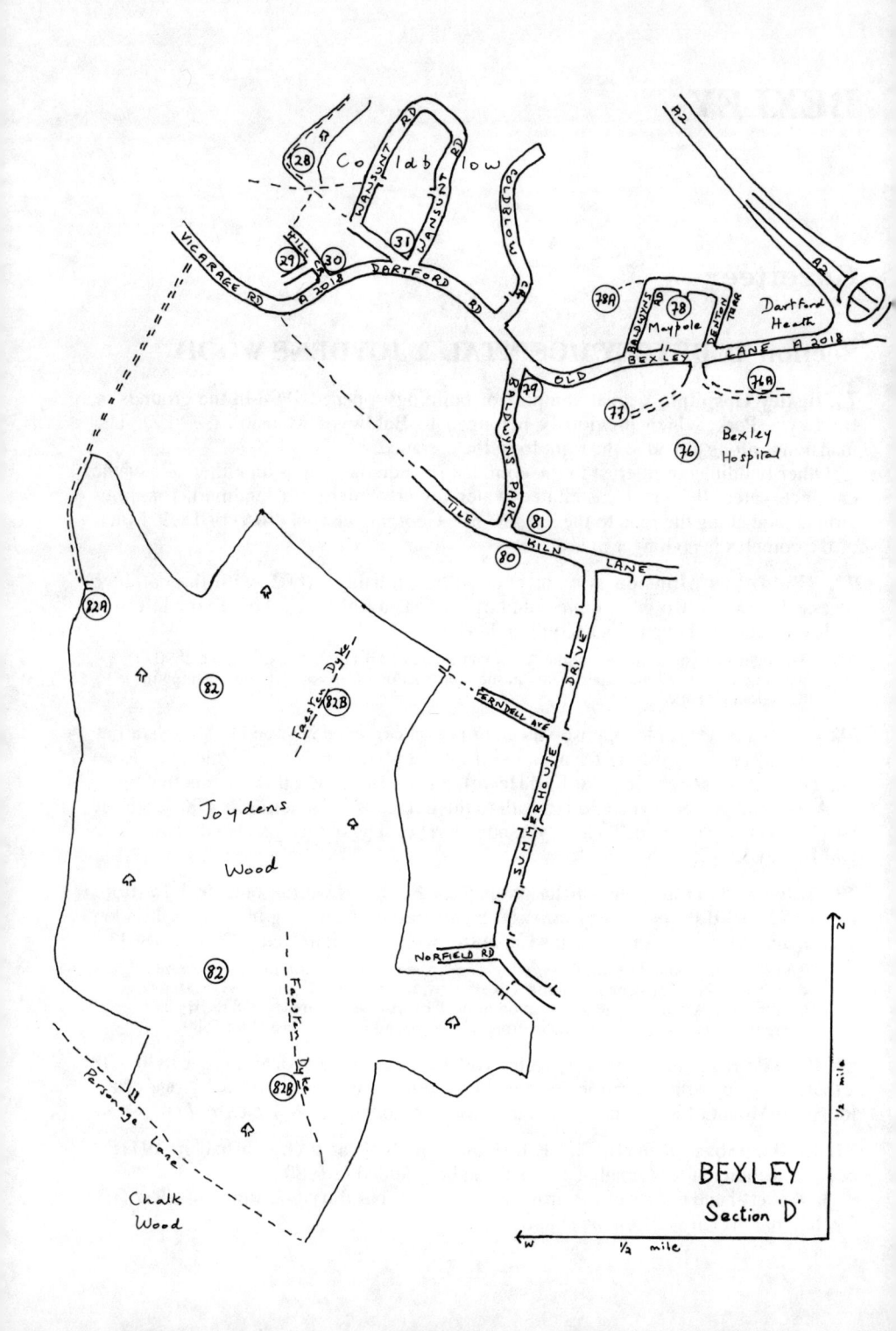

82. *Joydens Wood. A really vast area of woodland, parts of which are ancient woodland. There is a wide variety of trees, including belts of conifers which date from the time the wood was acquired by the Forestry Commission in 1956. There are also open glades of heather and bracken, as well as several ponds.
   It is now managed by The Woodland Trust, and was opened to the public in 1988.
   The **Keeper's Cottage (82A)** is a building of 1888, and bears the letters 'GVHM' (Sir George Vesey Holt Mackenzie, who owned Mount Mascal at the time.)
   Running north / south through the wood is *Faesten Dyke (82B)*, a Saxon defensive linear earthwork. It consists of an embankment with a ditch alongside to the west, certain sections being quite well preserved. It is considered that it may possibly have been created by the Anglo-Saxon leader Hengist after he had defeated the Britons at the Battle of Crayford c457.

   The wood contains a number of **deneholes**, or vertical shafts which open out into small chambers at the bottom; they were used for extracting chalk, mainly for use as fertiliser on the surrounding fields. They were dug mainly between the 17th century and the end of the 19th century, and all known examples have now been blocked. (Other deneholes have been found nearby just north of Joydens Wood, and to the west of the street called Baldwyns Park.)

*There is a network of well surfaced footpaths through the Wood, and it is sensible not to stray too far from these. There is also a network of bridle paths, particularly on the western side, and in fact many of the fields surrounding the wood are used by riding stables.*

*Great care should be taken if any shaft or depression, which could be an old denehole, is discovered, for the soil around could be highly unstable.*

*First time visitors are strongly recommended to acquire beforehand the leaflet 'A walk around Joydens Wood', either from the public library in Summerhouse Drive, or direct from The Woodland Trust, Autumn Park, Grantham, Lincs (phone 0476 74297), and to follow carefully the recommended walk.*

*The walk is about two miles long; it is quite hilly in parts, and it should be borne in mind that certain sections can become quite muddy at times. The walk passes the Faesten Dyke at two places.*

*The walk starts and ends at the main entrance, which is located in Summerhouse Drive (near the junction with Norfield Road) on the eastern side, in the housing area called Joydens Wood. This is the only entrance readily accessible for visitors arriving by car.*

*Other entrances are: on the eastern side, at the end of Ferndell Avenue, off Summerhouse Drive; and on the western side, at the Keeper's Cottage, and at the end of Parsonage Lane (see North Cray 16). The Keeper's Cottage is near Mount Mascal Stables, at the end of a National Grid road leading from Dartford Road, Bexley. Visitors using the two entrances on the western side should bear in mind that quite a long walk, from any bus-stop or from any point where a car could be parked, is involved before the entrance is reached.*

*Visitors wishing just to see the Faesten Dyke should enter at the end of Ferndell Avenue, continue ahead for nearly 200 yards, then turn left along a broad path; after about 300 yards, having passed the back fences of some houses, turn right along another broad path. After about 200 yards you will see an impressive section of the Dyke to the left.*

*There is a pleasant public footpath running the full length of the western side of the wood, from Parsonage Lane to the Keeper's Cottage. Bear in mind that it can become very muddy, some stiles have to be negotiated, and you may be pestered by fierce sounding dogs from nearby riding stables.*

# BEXLEY

## Suggested Walks

*It is recommended that the two suggested walks be followed in conjunction with the Gazetteer and the maps, and that the Gazetteer be consulted at each location for a detailed description (all places in bold type are mentioned in the Gazetteer). Most locations described in Sections 'B' and 'C' of the Gazetteer are covered; some other locations have not been included, as they might add too much to the length of the walks. They follow a more or less circular route, so can be joined at any location.*
*Section 'A' is not included, as Hall Place needs a special visit and the gazetteer entry describes in detail a walk around the places of interest. Section 'D' is not included, as the locations are too far apart; the gazetteer entry for Joydens Wood gives information on walks through the Wood.*

**WALK No 1** (including Bexley High Street, Bourne Road, St Marys Church, North Cray Road, and Parkhurst). Distance approx two miles.

*NB. It is worth trying to make advance arrangements - see the gazetteer - to view the interiors of St Marys Church, the Baptist Church and St Johns Church. The walk begins and ends at Bexley Station. It sets out along the north side of the High Street and returns along the south side, identifying locations along each side; because the High Street is so narrow, it is often the case that there are better views of a building from the opposite side of the road. The High Street can be a dangerous place for pedestrians, so extreme care should be taken when crossing the road. The only proper pedestrian crossing is in Bourne Road, near the High Street end.*

SECTION 'B'. On leaving **Bexley Station (3)**, go down Station Approach to the High Street and cross to **Stylemans Almshouses (4)**. Bear right along the north side of the High Street, passing **no 57 (5)**, **Freemantle Hall (7)**, and **The Kings Head & nos 67/71 (8)**.

On reaching the junction with Bourne Road, turn left up to **Old Bexley Baptist Church (9)** - try to see the interior. Continue up Bourne Road, passing **Bexley Village Library (10)** and **Victoria Homes (11)**, until you reach **nos 66/70 (12)** (the former **Bexley National School**). Cross the road and return along the east side. You pass **nos 17/19 (14)** (former **Reffells Brewery**), **no 11 (15)**, the old **stables** for the **Kent Brewery** at **no 5 (16B)**, and **nos 1/3 (9A)**.

At the junction with the High Street, note the old **finger signboards (17)** above no 77a, and turn left. You pass **The Millers Arms (18)** and **no 85 (19)**, then continue under the railway viaduct to **Thomas Shearley Court (20)** and **Bexley Bridge (21)**. Beyond the bridge, pass **no 101 & nos 107/115 (22)**, **Brook Cottage (23A)** and **Highstreet House (23)**. Note the two sheds at the boundary with the churchyard.

Go into **St Marys Churchyard (25)**, proceeding under the **old lychgate,** to the **Church of St Mary (24)** - try to see the interior. Go to the end of the churchyard for a view (not very satisfactory) of the **Manor House (26C)**. Leave the churchyard by the far gate, and cross Manor Road straight into **St Marys Cemetery (26E)**. Return to Manor Road and turn left, passing **Manor Cottage (26B)** and **Manor Lodge (26A)**. At the junction, turn left along **North Cray Road**.

Continue to the junction with Vicarage Road; note, around the junction, **no 33 (27)** and **St Marys Cottage (33)**, and beyond the junction **The Coach & Horses (34)**. Cross North Cray Road and return, passing **nos 30/34 (36)** around the junction. Note the group of houses from **16 North Cray Road** to **106/8 Bexley High Street (37)**. Continue along the High Street, going up the driveway to see **Clarendon Mews (38)**, return and pass **Cray House (39)**. You now reach the forecourt between **The Old Mill (40)** (look at the interior) and Bexley Bridge.

Go under the viaduct, then note **Mill Row (41)** to the left. Continue, passing **nos 82/84 (42)**, **nos 76/80 (44)**, **The George (43)**, **nos 48/68 (44)**, **The Railway Tavern (45)** and **nos 34/36 (46)**, which is just before Station Approach. Continue along the High Street, passing **Oxford Terrace (47)** until you reach the **United Reformed Church (48)**. Then cross to the **War Memorial (49)**.

SECTION 'C'. Walk alongside **Fair Field** to the **Church of St John the Evangelist (52)**; try to see the interior. Cross to the **Penfold hexagonal pillar box** opposite, and pass to the right of **Island House (53)** and Parkhurst Gardens. Continue along **Parkhurst Road** as it bears right, noting **nos 64/50 (54)** & **42/32 (55)** on the left. Return to Parkhurst Gardens and bear right along **Upton Road South**, noting **nos 234/240 (56)** on the left. Turn left down **Cross Lane (57)** back to Parkhill Road, then turn left.

SECTION 'B'. Continue until you reach **Park House (50)**, opposite the War Memorial. Bexley High Street begins here; note **nos 1/3 & 7/9 (51)**, then pass Stylemans Almshouses and cross to Station Approach and back to Bexley Station.

**WALK No 2** (including Blendon, Bexley Woods, the Shuttle Riverway and Hurst). Distance approx two and a half miles.

*The walk begins and ends at the Three Blackbirds pub. Bear in mind that Bexley Woods and sections of the Shuttle Riverway can at times become quite muddy.*

SECTION 'C'. From the **Three Blackbirds (64)**, cross the road and bear left for **Jays Cottages (63)**. Return on the south side of the road, pass **West Lodge (65)** and continue to the second roundabout - note on the opposite side of the roundabout **Chapel House** *(see Welling 10)*. Turn left down Penhill Road, and pass **Blendon Methodist Church** (the old and new churches) **(66)** and **St James Church (67)**.

On reaching Penhill Bridge, turn left along the **Riverside Walk (70)** of the Shuttle Riverway. At the second bridge, turn right down Crofton Avenue to see **Hurst Place (71)** and return to the Riverside Walk. Continue and you will come to **Bexley Woods (59)**; make a detour into the Woods, then follow the river out to Parkhill Road. Cross to **Riverdale Road (58)**, then return to Parkhill Road and turn right.

Parkhill Road becomes **Bridgen Road**; note **nos 1/13 (60)** on the right. The road then becomes Blendon Road. Take the next road on the right, which is **Arcadian Avenue (61)**, and follow the crescent round, turn left into Woodside Lane. At the junction with Blendon Road, turn right, noting **no 44 (62)** (the former Bridgen National School) on the corner, then continue back to the Three Blackbirds.

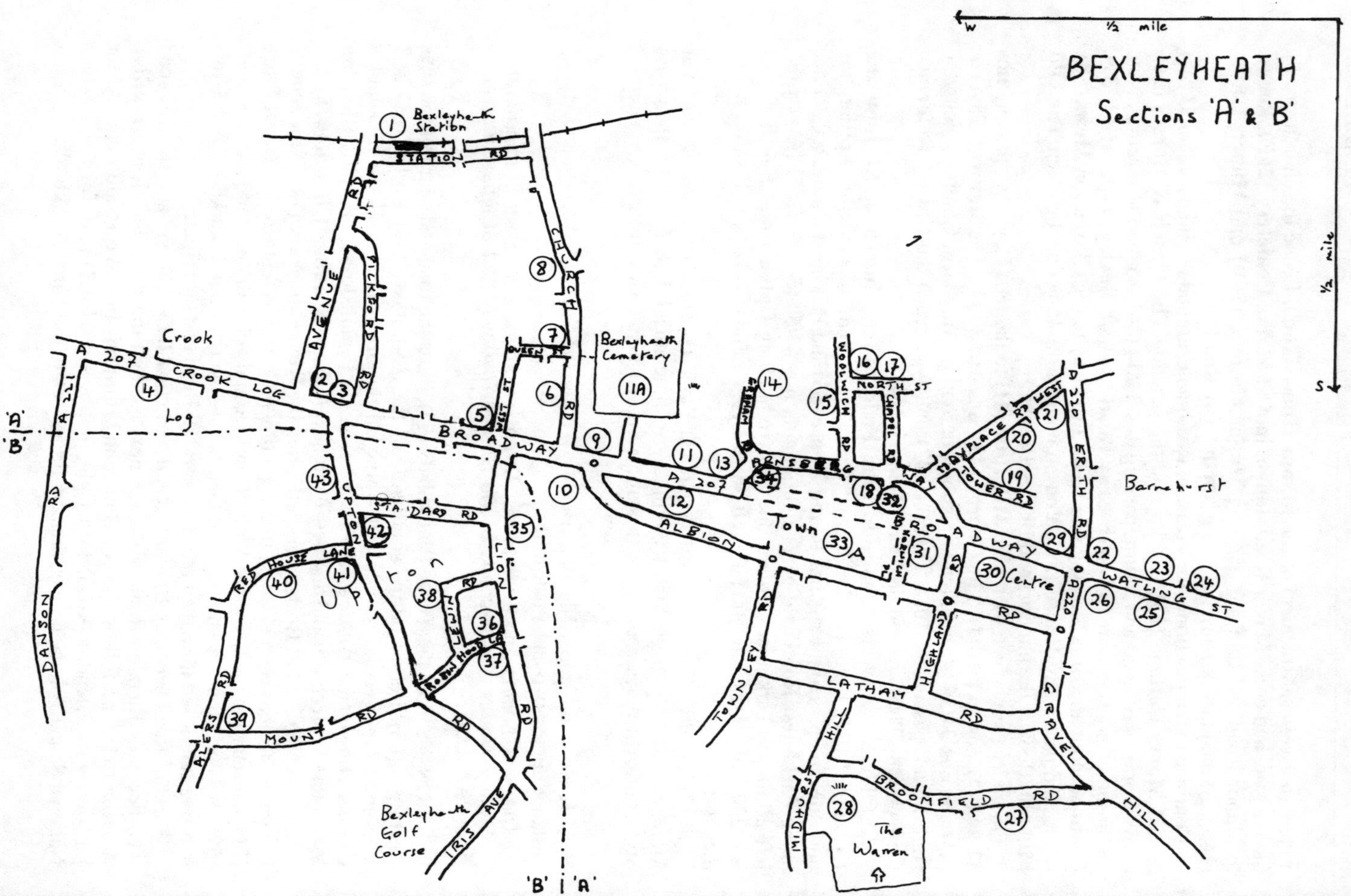
BEXLEYHEATH
Sections 'A' & 'B'
W
½ mile
S
½ mile
Bexleyheath Station
STATION RD
AVENUE RD
PILKFORD RD
CHURCH RD
QUEEN ST
WEST ST
Bexleyheath Cemetery
Crook
A 207
CROOK LOG
Log
A 221
DANSON RD
BROADWAY
A 207
ARNSBERG WAY
GRESHAM RD
WOOLWICH RD
NORTH ST
CHAPEL RD
MAYPLACE RD WEST
TOWER RD
ERITH RD
A 220
Barnehurst
ALBION RD
Town
Centre
NORWICH PL
HIGHLAND RD
WATLING ST
LATHAM RD
TOWNLEY RD
GRAVEL HILL
BROOMFIELD RD
MIDHURST HILL
The Warren
STANDARD RD
UPTON RD
Upton
RED HOUSE LANE
LION RD
LEWIN RD
ROBIN HOOD LA
MOUNT RD
ALERS RD
IRIS AVE
Bexleyheath Golf Course
'A'
'B'
1
2
3
4
5
6
7
8
9
10
11
11A
12
13
14
15
16
17
18
19
20
21
22
23
24
25
26
27
28
29
30
31
32
33
34
35
36
37
38
39
40
41
42
43

# BEXLEYHEATH

## Introduction

Bexleyheath forms, together with Welling, a long plateau between the higher ground of Shooters Hill to the west and the lower ground of Crayford and Dartford to the east.
To the south of Bexleyheath, the escarpment falls quite sharply to the River Shuttle, Bexley Village and the River Cray. The southern boundary is effectively defined by Rochester Way, which was first constructed in 1926, though much widened in recent years; from here the Woolwich Building Society head office, the Swallow Hotel, and the protuberances on top of the Broadway Shopping Centre can be seen conspicuously perched on the escarpment.
The area also embraces the old hamlet of Upton, tucked away south of the main road to Welling. To the north of the railway line is a vast, rather unrelieved area of predominantly interwar housing.

## The beginnings

The main road through Bexleyheath follows quite closely, though slightly to the north, the route of Watling Street, the Roman road from London to Dover. There is no evidence of a Roman settlement, though in Iris Avenue in 1973 there were important finds from a Roman cremation.
In 1800 Bexley Heath (as it was then spelt) was a tract of common heathland along the Dover Road - it was much like large areas of Dartford Heath look now. The Golden Lion was the most prominent building, and the area was inhabited by squatters mostly working in the expanding fabric-printing industry at Crayford.
Local landowners reacted to this growing settlement by pressing for the enclosure of the heath. The enclosure awards were made in 1819 and 1820, and Bexley New Town (as it was sometimes known) began to develop quite rapidly, focussed around the Market Place which was at the junction of Mayplace Road and Broadway. The main stimulus was still the textile industry at Crayford.

## The development of Bexleyheath

By 1860 there were churches and pubs; housing was concentrated along Broadway, Watling Street to the east, the Mayplace Road triangle, and in roads to the north like Chapel Road, Woolwich Road, and Church Road.
In 1894 the spelling of Bexley Heath was officially changed to Bexleyheath. In 1895 the railway arrived, with the station located just west of the central area; by this time housing (including large houses, some still surviving) had begun to develop in this area in roads like Pickford Road and Avenue Road, and along Crook Log.

Houses along Broadway were converted to shops; many of the present-day shops retain their Victorian upper floors.

Tramways linking Bexleyheath with Erith and Woolwich started in 1903, and with Dartford in 1905; by then Bexleyheath had begun to merge with Welling to the west and Crayford to the east.

Bexleyheath lost its location on the main London to Dover road in 1926, when Rochester Way was built to the south. Its town centre has however since the 1980s become a major shopping and civic centre.

## The Town Centre

The town centre is now in the course of redevelopment. The pedestrianised area around the central part of Broadway, bounded by the recently constructed relief roads of Arnsberg Way to the north and Albion Road to the south, is characterised by a number of large buildings of the 1980s and early 1990s - the Broadway Shopping Centre, the Civic Offices, Bexley Magistrates Court, the Central Library, Swallow Hotel, the new Police Station (nearing completion), and several large car parks. They are mostly in a subdued modernist style with vernacular overtones, and the overall effect is rather uninspired.

The only two modern buildings which convey some sense of excitement are smaller - the United Reformed Church and the post-modernist Lex Garage; though there are two quite dramatic large buildings on the fringes of the area - the Head Office of the Woolwich Building Society, and the Asda Store.

Only a few older buildings will survive redevelopment - the Clock Tower and two pubs, The Kings Arms & Prince Albert. Other older buildings - Bexleyheath Police Station of 1907, the Duke of Edinburgh pub and the adjoining terrace of three mid 19th century cottages, the old Athenaeum (in the Bexleyheath Shopping Hall), and Trading World (the old Co-op store of 1956) - are scheduled for demolition. The paved area to the east of the Clock Tower was the site of the Market House, an early 19th century building which was until demolition in 1990 after fire damage the oldest building in the Town Centre.

At the eastern edge of the town centre, in Watling Street, a number of early 19th century buildings have, quite amazingly, survived.

## Upton

Upton is an old hamlet, tucked away to the south of the main road from Bexleyheath to Welling, and still remains somewhat rural in atmosphere, with many older houses.

Outstanding amongst these is The Red House, built in 1859 by Philip Webb for William Morris; this was a highly influential building in the history of British architecture, and was the forerunner of the Arts & Crafts movement.

Many of the roads of Upton - Upton Road, Red House Lane, Lion Road, Robin Hood Lane, Mount Road - still largely follow the course of the winding lanes of the early 19th century. The distinct identity of Upton, much older than the rest of Bexleyheath, can still be discerned.

# BEXLEYHEATH

## Gazetteer

### Section 'A' BROADWAY & CROOK LOG

**1. Bexleyheath Station.** The present rather ordinary station building is of 1931. The footbridge is of 1924. The station was originally opened in 1895.

**2. 2 Avenue Road,** an extraordinary house, probably c1880; it has a Gothic porch topped by an amazing octagonal turret with a conical roof.

**3. *Crook Log.** This prominently located pub is early 19th century in appearance, but may contain some 18th century structure. The extension at an angle to the east is also early 19th century, though much altered.

**4. 4/6 Crook Log,** a pair of the 1880s with fine decorative features.

Adjacent is the **Polo Bar,** formerly called the Upton Hotel and The Jolly Draymen, a pub basically of 1870 though much altered.

**5. Golden Lion,** Broadway. There are records of a coaching inn on this site going back to c1730, the oldest in the area. The present handsome and prominent building of 1901, with its oriels over the corner entrance and on the main road, heralds the approach to Bexleyheath from the west.

**6. 20 Church Road.** An exceptional house, probably of the 1870s, in an Arts & Crafts style.

**7. The Volunteer,** Church Road. A pleasing early 19th century pub, with three gables on the frontage along Queen Street.

**8. Upland School,** Church Road. A large and rather grand building built in 1895 for the Bexley School Board; the central pediment and the spandrels around the archway below are profusely carved.

**9. *Trinity Chapel.** The frontage of this Baptist Church of 1868 by Habershon & Pite has a powerful impact in its key location. It is almost extravagantly classical, with an Italianate doorcase and four tall Corinthian pilasters surmounted by a great dentilled pediment enclosing a circular window. There are tall round-headed windows along both sides. Pleasing interior, with a fine gallery and wooden roof.

**10. The War Memorial Garden** contains memorials for both world wars. A stone is inscribed: 'This stone is erected adjacent to the site of the original Chapel of Ease of Christ Church Bexleyheath. Chapel erected 1836, demolished 1878, steeple erected 1851, demolished 1928'. *(See below.)* Some old gravestones have survived at the southern end of the garden.

**11. *Christ Church.** A tall and bulky but very grand and imposing Victorian Gothic ragstone church of 1877 by William Knight. It can be readily seen that a central steeple had been intended. Note the fine detailing in the chancel windows, the west window, and the rose windows in the transepts.

> The first Anglican church in Bexleyheath was the Chapel of Ease (to the parish church of Bexley), built 1836 in what is now the War Memorial Garden *(see 10)*. It was enlarged with a steeple in 1851.
> The parish of Bexleyheath was formed in 1866. The new parish church was begun in 1872 and largely completed by 1877. The old chapel was demolished in 1878, though the steeple was left standing until 1928.

The **interior** may perhaps be found disappointing after the grandeur of the exterior. *(The church is normally open weekdays 1200 to 1315, otherwise telephone 081-303 3260 or 303 9509.)* The nave is lofty but stark and bare; the chancel is more imposing, with its shafts springing upwards. The green painted roof is postwar.

To the south-west of the church is the **Pincott Memorial**, an obelisk of 1878 to the first vicar, William Pincott; the fountain has disappeared. It was originally sited where the Clock Tower is now *(see 32)*.

To the north-east is the former **Vicarage**, a rather macabre Gothic house of 1868 by Ewan Christian, enlivened by some nice diaper pattern brickwork.

Behind the church and to the west is **Bexleyheath Cemetery (11A)**. The cemetery, opened 1879, has many late 19th century tombs in the southern part, but it has no landscape interest. It does however, together with a small adjoining park, form a welcome green space close to the shopping centre.

**12. Kwik Save supermarket**, 167 Broadway. This is a conversion of the former Broadway cinema of 1929.

**13. ASDA store.** This building of 1988 seems quite sensational in this part of Broadway, with its spectacular sweep of dark glass above bands of yellow and red brick, and its startling green signs.

**14. Bexleyheath School Sixth Form Centre**, Graham Road. The long, low-lying building on the right as you enter the Bexleyheath School grounds is the original **Bexleyheath National School** of 1883.

**15. *62 Woolwich Road**, formerly called Orchard House. An attractive weatherboarded early 19th century house in an isolated location, on the edge of school playing-fields. There are local stories that it was moved on wheels to this site from Mayplace Road in 1864.

**16. 65/67 Woolwich Road**, formerly known as Albion Villas. A fine pair of concrete houses of 1866 by Joseph Tall, with rusticated ground floors. These are amongst the earliest surviving concrete houses.

**17. Bethany Hall**, North Street, was built as the Wesleyan Chapel in 1860. It is an intriguing pedimented building, with polychrome Gothic doors and windows. It closes the view down Chapel Road from the Town Centre.

**18. United Reformed Church**, Geddes Place. A quite striking modern church of 1988 with a steeply sloping slate roof, out of which an odd quadrangular dormer projects. Note how the large brick crucifix is incorporated into the design of the north front. It was built on the site of the Congregational Chapel of 1854 (demolished in 1987).

The interior is lofty, with great wooden beams in the roof *(it can be seen readily through the windows, otherwise contact 0322 527831)*.

**19. The Foresters Homes**, Tower Road. This is a pleasing complex of 1975, surrounded by large grassed grounds, a remarkable oasis in this location; the gates are of 1962. The original almshouses on the site were built 1873-75 by the Ancient Order of Foresters.

**20. 65/83 Mayplace Road West.** This group of cottages of the 1860s are mainly stuccoed, and some have nice trellised porches.

**21. Jolly Millers**, 111 Mayplace Road West. An attractive pub c1860, much altered.

**22. \*Woolwich Building Society** Corporate Headquarters. A great irregular vernacular pile, with echoes of the Hillingdon Civic Centre, built 1989 by Broadway Malyan. It is basically of yellow stock brick, topped by great tiers of staggered red roofs receding upwards.

A rather heavy pedimented entrance porch leads into a soaring atrium the full height of the building, with glazed lifts and great oak beams at the top. Hanging on the side walls are tall hand-woven silk tapestries by Heidi Lichterman - to the right **A Walk into the Morning** 1988, and to the left **After the Storm** 1990.

Behind the main building is a complex of more functional buildings of the 1960s, with bands of white tiles and glass.

**23. The Coach House**, 40 Watling Street, formerly known as Lord Hill. A pleasing pub, its present appearance probably c1815, but dating back in part to the late 18th century.

**24. Sherston Place**, 60/68 Watling Street, a nice terrace of 1843 with great blank arches set into the facades.

**25. 25/27 Watling Street**, an interesting group, early 19th century. Note the fine timber windowcases and the oriel to the east.

**26. Grove Lodge**, 15 Watling Street, an attractive stuccoed house, early 19th century.

**27. Broomfield Road.** The south side of this road was first developed in the 1890s. Two large houses remain from this time, nos 1 (called Warren Wood) and 25, both with tile-hung upper floors, and looking sedate amidst the later development around.

**28. The Warren**, Broomfield Road. This green oasis is quite evocative. A large grassed area is backed by a tree-lined ridge, on which a grassed plateau overlooks dense woodland descending steeply to the A2.

**29. The Prince Albert**, 2 Broadway, a pleasant pub rounding the corner with Erith Road, probably mid 19th century. Note the fine timber-framed windows on the upper floor.

**30. Civic Offices**, a sprawling building of red brick with black slate tile inserts. The approach to the Council Chamber is through the central entrance. At the western end is the Information Office.

Opposite the western end of the complex is the **Duke of Edinburgh** pub, probably c1848, and an adjoining terrace of three cottages of 1845, **40/44 Broadway** (known as William Place), all due for demolition.

Opposite the eastern end is the **Lex Garage**, a jolly post-modernist building of 1991.

**31. Bexleyheath Shopping Hall.** A not very attractive mall, due for demolition. But it incorporates to the rear a brick hall, which was built in 1848 as a public hall, originally called **The Athenaeum**; it can be clearly seen from Norwich Place alongside.

**32. Clock Tower,** in red brick, built in 1911 to commemorate the coronation of George V. Though squat and heavy, it is worth noting the detailing. The lower storey is on a rusticated stone podium, and the second storey has niches flanked by double Ionic pilasters. All four sides are the same, except that to the west there is a classical stone doorcase (which in fact leads into an electricity sub-station), and in the niche above, a bust of George V by John Ravera 1990, which is a replica of the original.

**33. Broadway Shopping Centre,** by Fitzroy Robinson & Partners 1983, a massive block dominating the Town Centre. It has layers of steeply pitched red tile cladding on the sides; and these are echoed in the series of protuberances with steeply pitched red tiled roofs on the open car park on top, which are so conspicuous when viewed from the south.

The car park on the top deck provides panoramic *views stretching from Shooters Hill in the west to Dartford Bridge in the east; to the south, against the backcloth of Joydens Wood, can be seen the landmarks of the Water Tower of Bexley Hospital and the spire of St Johns Church, Bexley.

The shopping mall itself is garish and metallic; it is softened to some extent by the central square with its tropical plants, but this is often used for displays.

Outside the west entrance is a sculpture, **Family Outing**, by John Ravera 1985.

**34. The Kings Arms**, 156 Broadway, an elegant pub c1845 rounding the corner with Arnsberg Way.

# BEXLEYHEATH

## Gazetteer

### Section 'B' UPTON

**35. 59/75 Lion Road.** In this group, note, from north to south:
   **The Royal Standard,** no 59, a pleasant and harmonious pub, rebuilt in 1910; it effectively closes the view along Standard Road.
   **Raleigh Villa,** no 67, a large house c1880, with all sorts of ornamental flourishes.
   **Brooklands Guest House,** no 75, a fine large house of the 1880s, with chevron decoration over porch and windows, and diaper pattern brickwork on the side wall.

**36. Robin Hood & Little John.** This pub has a very rural look; it was built c1852, though it has been much altered. Note the bizarre inn-sign.

**37. *80 Lion Road,** formerly called Wye Lodge. This was probably a farm building, possibly as old as the 17th century, and certainly the oldest building in the Bexleyheath area. It was extended when converted to a house in the 19th century, and much altered during restoration in the 1950s. Note the old well in the yard.

**38. Lewin Road.** The first houses in this short road were built on the west side c1852. Note in particular **nos 9/15**, with their round-headed windows reaching down almost to ground level.
   At the end is **Robin Hood Lane**, an old lane which retains considerable atmosphere as it winds steeply down from Lion Road to Upton Road.

**39. *Royal Oak**, Mount Road. An old-established pub, its present weatherboarded appearance probably of 1863, and highly attractive. There was a building on the site by 1800, and it has been a pub since c1827. It is also called Polly Cleanstairs - the name can be seen on the inn-sign and over the entrance.

**40. ***The Red House**, Red House Lane. Philip Webb's first building, specially built to the specifications of the young William Morris in 1859. The interior contains wonderful furnishings and decorations, many by Morris himself.
   The house was the forerunner of the Arts and Crafts movement, and pioneered the 19th century vernacular revival; whilst retaining Gothic forms, it used traditional building materials and design features. Its influence on subsequent housing design has been considerable, and many of its features may now seem commonplace. It remains an outstanding architectural masterpiece, and is a wonderful place to visit.

The site was chosen for its rural character amidst orchards, yet accessible from London. At the time there were only a few houses in the hamlet of Upton, and William Morris made the journey by rail to Abbey Wood, followed by a three mile drive through the fields to his house. His pre-Raphaelite friends, including Edward Burne-Jones, Charles Faulkner and Dante Gabriel Rossetti, helped with its interior design. Morris stayed there for only five years until moving to Queen Square, Bloomsbury.

The house is in a large garden, with some of the original apple trees; the house and the garden were intended as an integrated design. The house forms an L-shape, with north and west ranges; Morris originally intended to complete the square with east and south ranges as a residence for Burne-Jones.

The red brick front wall, with its piers and wooden gate, is contemporary with the house, as are the adjoining stables and coach-house, with long sweeping roofs and tiny dormer. The blue plaque by the gate says: 'Red House, built 1859-60 by Philip Webb architect for William Morris poet and artist, who lived here 1860-65'. It is not possible to see the house itself properly from the street, though in the winter there are views of the upper floors of both ranges.

*It is open to the public on the first Saturday afternoon and Sunday afternoon in each month (except January), but only by prior arrangement. Write to Mrs D. Hollamby, The Red House, Red House Lane, Bexleyheath (enclosing a stamped addressed envelope) to ask for permission to view (telephone 081-303 8808).*

The overwhelming external impact of the house is provided by the accentuated Gothic detail, intended to recall medieval romanticism. It is of deep red brick, and the features are quite asymmetrical; the roofline is irregular, and the roofs are very steeply pitched. The windows have a rhythmic pattern, but follow the demands of the internal room arrangement; the window styles are manifold - Gothic lancet, Arts and Crafts circular, Georgian segmental (often under a Gothic arch).

The north front is notable for its imposing full-height entrance porch, with Gothic arches over the entrance and over the two small windows above. To the left are three windows under a hipped dormer and then a great chimneystack, and to the right three lancets under a high gable.

Within the porch note the text in a strange medieval-style alphabet carved in the brick over the doorway: 'Dominus custodiet exitum tuum et introitum tuum'. The window panels in the front door have modern abstract designs in glass mosaic by Anthony Holloway representing 'The Four Seasons'.

The west front with its great roof seems still more powerful, particularly to the left with the towering chimneystack alongside a strange rhomboidal oriel, which corbels and fans out from the buttress below.

The rear view from the garden to the south-east is the most picturesque, with a rustic well-head set in front of a staircase tower in the angle of the L-shape. The well-head has a tall conical cap supported on massive oak posts. The staircase tower has a pyramid roof topped by a tiny cap with a weather-vane engraved 'WM 1859'. To the right the rear of the north wing has a row of circular windows at upper floor level, and a garden porch with a Gothic entrance arch.

The ***interior** is equally interesting. It is preserved in the style of the original as much as possible and reasonable, bearing in mind that it is still a family home.

The **hall** has a settle adorned by unfinished paintings by Morris of scenes from the Nibelungenlied. The reverse of the front door was painted by Morris with geometrical patterns.

To the right is the **living-room** (originally the dining-room), which has a huge red lacquered dresser designed by Philip Webb. The fireplace has an intriguing brick pattern; some of the tiles were designed by Morris.

In the passage to the left the windows have small painted panes by Morris and Burne-Jones; the figurative panels representing 'Love' (in a red tunic) and 'Fate' (in a green robe) are later inserts.

The **staircase** ahead is of oak, with slim newel posts; the ceiling above the staircase is painted in bold geometrical and curvilinear patterns which were pricked out in the wet plaster.

The **drawing-room** on the first floor is the most impressive in the house; it is lit by the three lancets on the north front and the oriel on the west front. In this room is the famous brick fireplace with its great hood bearing the motto 'Ars longa vita brevis' where it meets the ceiling.

But the room is dominated by the enormous settle, which had been designed by Morris and was brought from his former studio in Red Lion Square; a ladder leads to a platform above the settle, which serves as a minstrels gallery and gives access to the roof loft. (A cupboard door panel painted by Rossetti representing 'Dante's Amor' which was on the settle is now in the Tate Gallery.) The settle is flanked by three wall paintings by Burne-Jones based on the wedding of Sire Degravaunt, a medieval romance by Froissart, but intended to symbolise Morris's own marriage; seven painted panels were projected, but only these three were completed.

**41. *Hogs Hole Cottages,** 1/9 Red House Lane and 44 Upton Road (which was originally two cottages). A very attractive long terrace of whitewashed cottages. They are basically of 1819, though they may incorporate some 18th century structure.

**42. 25 Upton Road**, an amazing house of 1870 in Tudor style, of brick with massive stone dressings. It is flanked on either side by houses with Gothick upper floor windows.

**43. Upton Day Hospital**, 14 Upton Road, originally known as Bexley Cottage Hospital. The original building of 1884 is small and vernacular, with a half-timbered jettied upper floor; there is a long later extension to the south. A few doors away is:

**8 Upton Road**, a one-storey brick cottage orné of 1856. Note the Gothic tracery on the round-headed windows, and the thatched roof with its tiny pointed dormer.

# BEXLEYHEATH

## Suggested Walks

*It is recommended that the two suggested walks be followed in conjunction with the Gazetteer and the maps, and that the Gazetteer be consulted at each location for a detailed description (all places in bold type are mentioned in the Gazetteer). Most locations described in Section 'A' and all locations in Section 'B' of the Gazetteer are covered; a few other locations in Section 'A' have not been included, as they might add too much to the length of the walks. Both walks begin and end at Bexleyheath Station, though a shorter alternative using the Golden Lion pub is suggested. They follow a more or less circular route, so can be joined at any location.*

**WALK No 1** (including Broadway and the Town Centre). Distance approx three and a half miles (approx two and a half miles if begun and ended at the Golden Lion pub).

*NB. Try to time your programme or make an advance arrangement - see the gazetteer - to view the interior of Christ Church.*

SECTION 'A'. From **Bexleyheath Station (1)** proceed to Avenue Road and turn left. Continue, noting **2 Avenue Road (2)** on the left just before you turn left along the main road. (At this point a detour westwards to see the **Crook Log** pub **(3)** and return would add about 600 yards to the walk.) Note **4/6 Crook Log** and the **Polo Bar (4)** immediately on the left, and continue along Broadway until you reach the **Golden Lion (5)** on the left.

Proceed eastwards along Broadway and turn left along **Church Road**; note **no 20 (6)** and **The Volunteer (7)** on the left, then return to Broadway.

On reaching **Trinity Chapel (9)**, cross over to the **War Memorial Garden (10)**, then return. Continue to **Christ Church (11)** (try to see the interior), and note the **Pincott Memorial** in front and the **Vicarage** behind. Note **Kwik Save (12)** opposite.

Continue to **ASDA (13)**, then turn left along Arnsberg Way; you are now going along the north side of the pedestrianised Town Centre. Turn left up **Woolwich Road**, noting **no 62 (15)** on the left, and on the other side of North Street, **nos 65/67 (16)** on the right. Go down North Street to **Bethany Hall (17)**, then turn right along Chapel Road to the **United Reformed Church (18)** (the interior can be seen through the windows).

Continue along Arnsberg Way, then branch left up Mayplace Road West. Take a detour along Tower Road to see the **Foresters Homes (19)**. Note **65/83 Mayplace Road West (20)** and the **Jolly Miller (21)** on the right, then turn right down Erith Road to the **Woolwich Building Society** head office **(22)**; go into the atrium.

Turn left along **Watling Street,** noting the **Coach House (23)** and **Sherston Place (24)** on the left and **nos 25/27 (25)** and **Grove Lodge (26)** on the right. Return to the junction with Erith Street and go straight ahead along Broadway, noting the **Prince Albert (29)** on the right.

You are now entering the pedestrianised Town Centre. Note the **Civic Offices (30)** on the left, and the **Lex Garage** and the **Duke of Edinburgh** on the right. Continue, passing the **Bexleyheath Shopping Hall (31)** (which incorporates the old **Athenaeum** at the rear) on the left, until you reach the the **Clock Tower (32)** on the right. The entrance to the **Broadway Shopping Centre (33)** is opposite; take the lift to the top for the **views.**

Continue along Broadway, noting **The Kings Arms (34)** on the right at the junction with Arnsberg Way, until you are back at the Golden Lion. Continue for some distance, then turn right into Pickford Road and then along Avenue Road until you are back at Bexleyheath Station.

**WALK No 2** (including the hamlet of Upton and The Red House). Distance approx two and a half miles (approx one and a half miles if the walk is begun and ended at the Golden Lion pub).

*NB. It is best to follow this walk when you have made an advance arrangement - see the gazetteer - to view the interior of The Red House.*

SECTION 'A'. From **Bexleyheath Station (1)** proceed to Avenue Road and turn left. Continue, noting **2 Avenue Road (2)** on the left just before you turn left along the main road. (At this point a detour westwards to see the **Crook Log** pub **(3)** and return would add about 600 yards to the walk.) Note **4/6 Crook Log** and the **Polo Bar (4)** immediately on the left, and continue along Broadway until you reach the **Golden Lion (5)** on the left.

SECTION 'B'. From the Golden Lion, cross and walk down **Lion Road.** Note the **Royal Standard, Raleigh Villa** and **Clarendon Guest House (35)** on the left, and further down, **Robin Hood & Little John (36)** on the right, and beyond Robin Hood Lane, **no 80 (37).** Go down **Robin Hood Lane** and turn right up **Lewin Road (38),** noting **nos 9/15** on the left, then return to Robin Hood Lane and turn right.

At the junction with Upton Road, cross and continue along Mount Road until you reach the **Royal Oak (39)** on the right, then turn right up Alers Road which bears right to become Red House Lane. Proceed to **The Red House (40).**

On leaving The Red House, turn right and continue up Red House Lane, noting **Hogs Hole Cottages (41)** on the right before turning left along **Upton Road.** Note **no 25 (42)** on the right, and **Upton Day Hospital** and **no 8 (43)** on the left.

On reaching the main road, cross and walk along Pickford Road and then Avenue Road until you are back at Bexleyheath Station. Alternatively, turn right and continue until you are back at the Golden Lion.

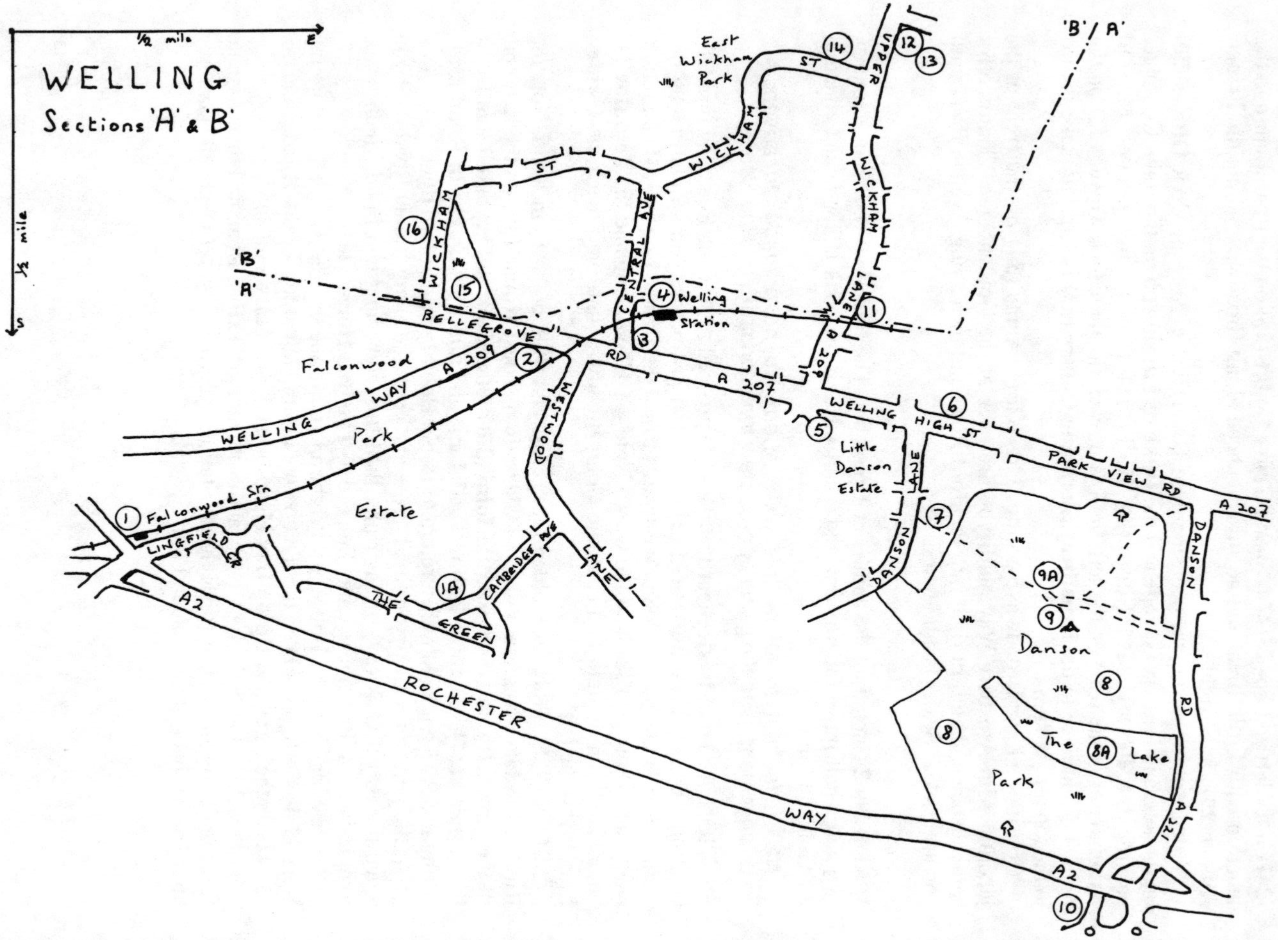
WELLING
Sections 'A' & 'B'
½ mile
E
½ mile
S
'B'
'A'
'B' / 'A'
East Wickham Park
UPPER WICKHAM LANE
WICKHAM ST
CENTRAL AVE
BELLEGROVE RD
A 209
A 207
Welling Station
Falconwood
WELLING WAY
Park
Estate
Falconwood Stn
LINGFIELD CR
WESTWOOD LANE
CAMBRIDGE AVE
THE GREEN
WELLING HIGH ST
Little Danson Estate
DANSON LANE
PARK VIEW RD
DANSON RD
A 221
Danson
The Lake
Park
ROCHESTER WAY
A2
1
1A
2
3
4
5
6
7
8
8A
9
9A
10
11
12
13
14
15
16

# WELLING

## Introduction

Watling Street, the old Roman road from London to Dover, now the A207 to Dartford, cuts through the shopping centre of Welling, which almost merges with the larger shopping centre of Bexleyheath to the east. To the north the area also embraces the old village of East Wickham and to the south the expanse of Danson Park. Shooters Hill with its woodlands looms above to the west, and the A2 forms a barrier to the south.

## Early history

Excavations in 1989 just west of the Guy Earl of Warwick pub in Park View Road provided evidence of a Roman settlement over four centuries, and there have been finds from Roman burials elsewhere on and around the Roman road in Welling.

East Wickham retains something of the atmosphere of an old village; it was a village with its own church in medieval times.

By the Tudor period there was a small settlement to the east of Nags Head Lane in Welling, and the estate of Danson, with a house on a site now under the lake, covered broadly the area of the present park. From Danson westwards the great expanse of West Wood linked up with the Shooters Hill Woods.

By 1800 the village of East Wickham extended along Wickham Street towards Shoulder of Mutton Green, and there was a manor house and a school, as well as farms and cottages. In Welling there were clusters of cottages on both sides of the main road, and Danson Park, with its mansion and lake, appeared much like it does today.

## East Wickham

The original village church of East Wickham, perched on its promontory overlooking the dried-up river bed of Wickham Lane, is very old. It was built in the early 13th century as a chapel to the original parish church at Plumstead.

The present winding course of Wickham Street (where an old farmhouse still survives) clearly indicates the old lane linking the village with its village green, known as Shoulder of Mutton Green, a mile away.

East Wickham has two modern churches by Thomas Ford in an Italian style, both with interesting interiors - St Michaels, built in 1933 in the churchyard behind the old village church, and St Marys, built in 1955 overlooking Shoulder of Mutton Green. In 1967 the old village church was transferred to the Greek Orthodox Church.

## Danson

The estate of Danson, with its old house, was acquired by John Boyd in the 1750s. He greatly enlarged the estate in the surrounding area, and commissioned Sir Robert Taylor to build a new villa, with interior decorations by Sir William Chambers; it was completed in 1768, originally called Danson Hill and now called Danson Mansion. The park was landscaped and a large lake created, covering the site of the old house.

The house and its grounds were acquired by Bexley Urban District Council in 1924. The grounds were opened as a public park in 1925, but unfortunately the Mansion has in recent years become derelict.

## Slow development of Welling

Welling was a hamlet, with inns serving as coach staging posts on the main road from London to Dover, until the late 19th century.

It remained largely rural, with inhabitants engaged primarily in agriculture, until the first world war. Even after the arrival of the railway in 1895, and after the introduction of a tram service linking Welling with Woolwich in 1903 and Dartford in 1905, development of housing was slow.

During the first world war the expansion of the Royal Arsenal at Woolwich led to settlements of huts for Arsenal workers filling much of the area between East Wickham and Welling.

## The modern suburb

In the 1920s, and much more so in the 1930s, the spread of housing in Welling and the growth of its population became very fast indeed; in fact, it showed one of the fastest rates of suburban growth in the London area.

In the 1920s the Little Danson Estate was developed on former Danson grounds to the west of the Park, and Bexley UDC built an estate in the angle formed by Wickham Street. To the south, Rochester Way was built in 1926. Welling High Street was widened and became a shopping centre in the 1930s.

In 1936 New Ideal Homesteads *(see Bexley 74)* promoted the opening of Falconwood Station, to serve their large new Falconwood Park Estate; it was on the site of part of Westwood Farm, which had replaced the old West Wood in the 1860s.

Since the last war housing development has been much slower, though the hut settlements in the area between East Wickham and Welling have been replaced.

# WELLING

## Gazetteer

### Section 'A' FALCONWOOD, HIGH STREET & DANSON

1. **Falconwood Station**, a station in art deco style, opened in 1936. It was partly funded by New Ideal Homesteads *(see Bexley 74)*, who were at that time building the Falconwood Park Estate to the east on the site of part of Westwood Farm. The estate has its own church and mock-Tudor shopping centre, **Falconwood Parade (1A)**, at The Green, where the farmhouse had been located.

2. **Welling Methodist Church**, Bellegrove Road. A brick building of 1935, with oddly shaped elongated windows. The interior *(contact 081-303 1452)* has a series of sharply angled arches, which in the nave lean inwards to follow the curve in the wall.

3. **Moon and Sixpence**. A pretty pub of 1897, formerly known as The Station Hotel. Note the strange corner turret, wooden balconies and decorative plasterwork.

4. **Welling Station**. The present building is of 1936, when the footbridge (which is open for use by the non-travelling public) was also built. The wooden shelter on the north (down) side remains from the original buildings when the station was opened in 1895.

5. **The Russian gun**. A Russian carronade (or short cannon of large bore), as used during the Crimean War 1854-56. It is set on a replica gun-carriage, and was placed here in 1987.

6. **17/35 Welling High Street**. This is the oldest group of buildings in the shopping centre, between two old pubs, the Rose and Crown (rebuilt 1870) and the Old Nags Head (rebuilt since the war). Note, from east to west:
   **The Rose and Crown**, a stuccoed pub of 1870.
   **No 21B**, a small one-storey shellfish shop, basically 19th century and retaining to the side double doors from its former use as a blacksmiths forge.
   **Nos 23/25**, early 19th century but considerably altered.
   **Nos 31/35**, basically 18th century with a mansard roof.

7. **Church of St John the Evangelist**. A basic but spacious Gothic brick church of 1926, in a fine position off a lane leading into Danson Park. The interior has a barrel roof *(contact the Vicarage, Danson Lane, next door, or ring 081-303 1107)*.

**8. *Danson Park.** A large and grand (but rather bare) park. Its focal point is Danson Mansion *(see below)*, on an elevated site overlooking a grassed expanse sweeping down to **The Lake (8A)**, which is nearly half a mile in length. The park was landscaped and the lake created c1770, in the style of Capability Brown. There are small woodland copses at the northern and southern edges.

> The Danson estate goes back at least to the 13th century; a substantial house was first built here probably during the 17th century. From 1698 to 1734 it was occupied by John Styleman, who founded the almshouses in Bexley Village *(see Bexley 4)*.
> 
> The House and its farmlands were acquired in the 1750s by John Boyd, owner of a West Indian plantation and (like Styleman) a Director of the East India Company. He commissioned Sir Robert Taylor to build a larger house, with internal decorations by Sir William Chambers; it was called Danson Hill, and was completed in 1768.
> 
> The grounds were landscaped c1770. The design included damming a stream to form a great lake, which covered the site of the old house, and converting a cottage beyond the lake to become Chapel House *(see 10)*.
> 
> A Doric temple by Chambers which used to be at the lakeside, near the site of the present boathouse (which is of 1964), is now at The Bury, an 18th century mansion at St Pauls Walden, near Stevenage.
> 
> The house, by then called Danson Mansion, and its grounds were acquired by Bexley UDC in 1924. The grounds were opened as a public park in 1925; the Mansion was initially used partly as a museum and also for functions, but since 1970 it has unfortunately become derelict.

The road entrance is from Danson Road, but there is an agreeable pedestrian approach through the handsome gates of 1929 at the corner of Park View Road and Danson Road.

To the north-west of the mansion are the old Stables *(see 9A)* c1800. Opposite the mansion is a formal Old English Garden.

The lake is used for boating at the eastern end, and the western end has become a sort of wildlife refuge. Beyond the western end is a rock garden with two ponds, linked by a stream which flows into the lake.

**9. \*\*\*Danson Mansion.** A fine mansion in Palladian style in the centre of Danson Park; it was built 1763-68 by Sir Robert Taylor.

It is in very poor and derelict condition, and is at present in the course of restoration by English Heritage. It is cut off from the park by fences and hedges, though quite good views can be obtained over the fencing.

The entrance front, facing north, is impressive and dignified, approached by a grand wide flight of steps with balustrades. The doorcase is by Sir William Chambers; it is ornately decorated, with a woman's face and an urn. The front is surmounted by a large dentilled pediment enclosing a circular window.

The rear and the sides have full-height canted bays, though only the rear bay is in accordance with Taylor's original design; the side bays were heightened above the main floor level in the early 19th century.

> *There is no general public access to the interior, which is seriously damaged and dilapidated; however, it is possible that an occasional visit for a small group may be arranged, and it may be worth ringing the Borough Valuer, London Borough of Bexley, on 0181-303 7777, or the Local Studies Centre on 01322 526574, to check whether this is likely.*
> 
> *Much of the interior decorations, including ceilings, chimneypieces and cornices by Sir William Chambers, and the paintings by Charles Pavillon, have been removed from the site.*

In the **interior**, the layout is of four major rooms around a central oval staircase. The entrance hall is to the north, the dining room to the east, the saloon to the south, and the music room to the west.

The front door leads into a large entrance hall, which has a niche on either side and eight recesses scooped out just below the cornice.

To the left is the Dining Room, with frames from which the paintings by Charles Pavillon have been removed, and great glazed arched recesses to north and south.

The saloon, or Octagon, which fits into the canted bay facing south, has beautiful views down to the lake. The rich and intricate ceiling decorations and palmette frieze below have survived more or less complete. In a corridor leading back to the entrance hall is a classical relief on an upper wall.

Next is the Music Room, or Library, facing west. The best remaining decorative features are two classical reliefs of a dancing woman surrounded by oak leaves. The bookcases set into the wall are probably 19th century. An organ of 1766 was removed from here in 1974 and is now at Hall Place *(see Bexley 1)*.

But the outstanding decorative feature of the house is the cantilevered stone staircase (with a fine wrought iron balustrade) in a tight oval well in the centre, top lit by a glazed oval dome. Around the upper floor landing is an oval balustrade with a colonnade of eight Ionic columns. A separate service staircase emerges abruptly on the landing just by the balustrade, and this looks rather strange.

The upstairs rooms do not, and never did, contain any important decorative features; the principal bedroom was over the octagon.

The *Stables (9A), to the north-west of the mansion, are large and impressive, with great archways in the centre and at the end of two projecting wings. Like the mansion, they are in poor condition. They were built c1800 to replace detached service blocks, linked to the mansion by quadrant walls, which had been part of Taylor's design.

10. *Chapel House, 497 Blackfen Road. This is a conversion c1770 of an older cottage to form a cottage orné. It has a Gothic door and windows with quatrefoil tracery, and a castellated turret-like chimney; a spire was added to make it look like a chapel which could be viewed from Danson Mansion. The facing was originally pink plaster, but is now roughcast.

Immediately to the south is what seems to be an old tomb, but is actually a stone and brick covering to an old well.

The house was converted to form part of the design for landscaping Danson Park *(see 8)*, but it can no longer be seen from the Mansion, and is now cut off from the Park by the A2.

# WELLING

## Gazetteer

### Section 'B' EAST WICKHAM

**11. Fosters School,** Upper Wickham Lane. A picturesque building of 1879, attractive front and rear, and still looking like a village school. Note the large gables, the thin rustic spire, the sweeping roof (with a quaint dormer on the east side), and the decorative detail.

It replaced a school of 1728 which was located further north near the old East Wickham church. On the front is a tablet of 1728 removed from the old school; the inscription reads in part 'for the perpetual education of 20 poor children ... in reading, writing and arithmetic'.

**12. \*\*Church of Christ the Saviour,** Upper Wickham Lane. A small early 13th century church, which has been a Greek Orthodox Church since 1967. It retains a single cell rectangular plan, ie without structural division between nave and chancel, and is the earliest complete church to survive without drastic alteration in the built-up area of South London.

> It was built as a chapel to the original parish church at Plumstead, and then became St Michaels Church, the parish church of East Wickham. A new and larger church was built in the churchyard in 1933, and eventually in 1967 the old church was transferred to the Greek Church; a number of interesting furnishings were moved to the new church at that time *(see 13).*

The church exterior is a mix of flint, stone, brick, tiles and rubble, evidence of how it has been patched and rebuilt over the centuries.

In the 18th century the church was extended westwards and the south wall rebuilt. In the early 19th century a south porch was added, later to become the modern vestry. In 1897 the roof was reconstructed and the bellcote added. Some original lancet windows remain in the north wall, and the square-framed windows are 15th century.

The **interior** *(contact 081-855 8116)* retains the outlines of a large medieval mural figure of St Michael on the north wall (other murals were destroyed in 1845). There is a fine iconostasis of 1977.

**13. St Michaels Church,** Upper Wickham Lane. A simple brick Byzantine basilica by Thomas Ford 1933, which is now the parish church of East Wickham. It is situated behind the original parish church, which was transferred to the Greek Orthodox Church *(see 12)* in 1967. The new church was modelled on San Apollinare Church, Ravenna (though without the campanile).

Some stones from an old building (probably the manor house of East Wickham), which were found during excavations for the foundations, have been incorporated in the two pillars outside the west front, and in the cross on the west wall.

The *interior *(contact the Vicarage next door, or ring 081-304 1214)* has some interesting furnishings transferred from the old church. These are mainly in the north aisle, and include, mounted on the wall, the fascinating brass c1325 to John and Maud de Bladigdone, and the 16th century Payne brasses, to William Payne 1568, his three wives (one brass missing) and three children. (The brasses were set into the floor of the sanctuary in the old church.) Also in the north aisle are three bells, the largest c1400 and the others of 1660 and 1897; and on a window sill, a brass plaque of 1763.

Other furnishings from the old church are the Jacobean lectern, Victorian funeral hatchments at the west end of both aisles, a coat of arms of Charles II on the front of the west gallery, and below, an iron chest, supposedly taken from a Spanish Armada galleon in 1588, but more probably 17th century.

The interior is however dominated by the splendid icon of Christ above the altar, painted in 1973 by Hieromonk Sophrony. Also note, amongst the modern furnishings, the stone font, and the stone pulpit with carvings.

The churchyard, with the two churches and many trees, is very pleasant.

**14. East Wickham Farm,** Wickham Street. The **farmhouse** survives; it has a facade of c1800, but its structure is much older. It is difficult to see, even in winter, because of the high fence and dense barrier of trees and bushes.

Also surviving are some outbuildings, alongside in Wickham Street, now in commercial use, and in Upper Wickham Lane, now used as riding stables.

**15. Shoulder of Mutton Green.** This is the old village green of East Wickham, though situated a mile away from the parish church and buildings of the old village.

> Shoulder of Mutton Green was acquired by the Metropolitan Board of Works in 1877. Like Plumstead Common and Bostall Heath, which were acquired at the same time, this followed attempts by Queens College Oxford, which owned all these lands, to deny public access.

**16. Church of St Mary the Virgin,** Wickham Street. A red brick church with Italian-style campanile, overlooking Shoulder of Mutton Green. The orientation of the church is to the west. It was built by Thomas Ford in 1955, and incorporates some pleasing works of art.

The tympanum over the entrance, which is deeply recessed, has a stylised sgraffito (or incised plaster engraving) by Augustus Lunn.

The *interior *(the church is often open, otherwise contact the Vicarage, Sandringham Drive, 081-856 0684 or 856 3500)* is in the style of Sir John Soane. A distinctive feature is the anthemion and palmette frieze, which runs all the way round under the ceiling and is repeated in other places too.

Over the altar, in a classical surround topped by angels, is a striking mural of The Ascension by Hans Feibusch. The stained glass windows in the sanctuary are of the Archangels Michael and Uriel. On the arches over the aisles is a series of paintings by Clare Dawson (an explanation of the paintings can be found on the east wall). The font, near the east wall, is imported and reputed to be 17th century.

The north aisle leads into the Chapel of St Thomas of Canterbury, its Gothic style contrasting with the general classical style of the interior. Note the fine carved reredos, and the Gothic window arches around the classical windows.

# SIDCUP

## Introduction

'If only I could get down to Sidcup', the vagrant Davies keeps repeating in Harold Pinter's play 'The Caretaker', and no doubt there is an implication that Sidcup is a rather ordinary suburb. This is far from true.

Until the arrival of the railway in 1866, Sidcup had a rural atmosphere with several large houses in large grounds. The area to the south of the High Street, where houses like Sidcup Place, Manor House and Frognal have survived, maintains this rural atmosphere. To the north of the High Street, the houses and their grounds may have disappeared and there is much modern infill, but the area retains a special late Victorian and Edwardian character.

The area of Sidcup covered by the gazetteers which follow is shown on the maps on pages 60 & 68. It includes the areas of Lamorbey and Blackfen to the north of the railway line, as well as Sidcup proper to the south of the line.

This introduction is extended to cover the areas further east, of Footscray and North Cray, in the Cray Valley below the Sidcup plateau.

## Early history

Though prehistoric implements have been found in the area, the earliest evidence of settlement came when the footings of a first century Roman bath-house were discovered during the building of the Bedensfield Estate at North Cray in 1956. Also, Roman pottery was found during construction of a water-main in 1991 further north on the east bank of the River Cray in Footscray Meadows, and it is considered that there was probably a Roman farmstead here.

There was a Saxon settlement at Foots Cray, and in Norman times both Foots Cray and North Cray were villages with their own churches.

By the end of the Tudor period there were houses with great estates at Lamorbey and The Hollies in the north, Frognal in the south, and Foots Cray, North Cray and Mount Mascal in the east. Great tracts of open space still remain in the area of these estates.

Between the mid 18th and the mid 19th century smaller villas began to appear throughout the area - some still exist, including Abbeyhill in the north; Sidcup Place and Manor House in the south; Vale Mascal, Loring Hall and Cray Hall in the east.

The main road from London to Maidstone passed through the area. It was improved by the New Cross Turnpike Trust in 1781, following the line of Main Road, Sidcup High Street, Sidcup Hill and Footscray High Street.

## Sidcup

Until the mid 19th century Sidcup was a hamlet around the Black Horse pub in the High Street. The road to Chislehurst started opposite and followed the line of Church Road and The Green. The first church was not completed until 1844.

Sidcup did not really develop until after the railway came, well to the north in Lamorbey, in 1866. The Park, Carlton Road, Main Road, Hatherley Road and Birkbeck Road were developed in the 1870s and 1880s. By 1901, when a much larger church was built, housing had covered most of the area between the High Street and the railway; the old hamlet around the Black Horse had expanded along the road on both sides, and a shopping centre had begun to form, which extended to the junction with Station Road.

Development of the area west of Station Road also began before 1900, enveloping Priestlands Wood and the estate of the demolished 18th century mansion Longlands, but was not completed until the interwar period.

Since the war the grounds of many late Victorian and Edwardian houses have been developed with blocks of flats and small estates. In Station Road, a number of large office blocks have been built; this road, winding from the High Street down to the station, is now an intriguing mixture of minor shopping parades, large postwar office blocks, Edwardian houses, and modern flats.

## Lamorbey & Blackfen

In the Tudor period there was a hamlet at Halfway Street, and two timber-framed houses still remain. There were also two substantial mansions - Lamienby-Goldwell, which became Lamorbey, substantially altered c1840; and Marrowbone Hall, which became The Hollies when replaced c1853. Lamorbey and The Hollies are still there, and much of their estates remains as open space.

Between these two estates runs Burnt Oak Lane, still following its old circuitous route. In this area Lamorbey's first church and first school were founded c1840, largely funded by the Malcolm family, who owned Lamorbey at the time. Further north Burnt Oak Lane swings round to join Days Lane, another old lane, in Blackfen, at a point where there was a hamlet at least by the early 18th century.

Sidcup Station was built to the south in 1866, and at that time the site would have been considered part of Lamorbey. But housing development in Lamorbey and Blackfen did not follow until after the first world war.

In the 1920s bungalows, many self-built, began to appear in Blackfen. But in the 1930s New Ideal Homesteads *(see Bexley 74)* transformed the area with a massive explosion of housing, and it was to become their heartland. The Montrose Park Estate and further east the Albany Park Estate were built just north of the railway line; and further north in Blackfen, the Marlborough Park and Penhill Park Estates.

These developments would make the whole area seem rather monotonous, were it not for the parklands of The Hollies and Lamorbey, as well as several surviving patches of woodland, particularly along the Shuttle Riverway. Also, the beautifully laid out estate around Willersley Avenue should be not be overlooked.

On the northern edge of the area, Blackfen Road was a country lane until housing came after the western part of the Danson Estate was sold in 1922; in the centre of Blackfen Road, around the pastiche pub The Woodman, is a minor shopping centre. Further north, the A2 was constructed in 1926, and was widened in the late 1960s.

## Footscray

Footscray was until quite recent times always spelt Foots Cray. It was a settlement in Saxon times, taking its name from its Saxon owner, Godwin Fot. The village developed during the Norman period around the point where the main road from London to Maidstone crossed the River Cray.

The first great house in the area was known as Pike Place, dating back at least to the 15th century; from then until c1676 it was owned by the Walsingham family, which included Sir Francis Walsingham, Secretary of State to Elizabeth I. It was demolished in the late 18th century; its location had been nearer the river and the church than its successor, Foots Cray Place.

The famous Palladian villa of Foots Cray Place was built c1754; although destroyed by fire in 1949, its site in Footscray Meadows can readily be detected. In 1822 it was bought by Sir Nicholas Vansittart, Chancellor of the Exchequer, later to become Lord Bexley. For most of the 19th century it was owned by the Vansittart family, who also owned the adjoining North Cray Place. The combined estate was vast, including much of the village and stretching north to Hurst, beyond the present railway line.

The population of the Footscray village grew in the late 19th century, after the railway came to Sidcup. There had been an important watermill (mostly used for paper making) on the river north of the bridge from 1767 to 1929; but the growth of industry did not come until the 1930s, after the opening of the Sidcup By-pass.

Though Footscray is sometimes considered part of Sidcup, its atmosphere is quite distinct; the High Street still looks like a village, with the River Cray running through, and has a number of important older buildings. Even modern buildings like Prospect House and Nexus House have Tudor-style overhanging upper floors in sympathy. To the south of the High Street, industry is dominant; but to the north the scene is rural with the vast Footscray Meadows, which were the former parklands of Foots Cray Place and North Cray Place, around the River Cray.

## The Cray Riverway

This signposted walkway follows the River Cray for much of its route, and the riverside walk for over a mile through Footscray Meadows is the most delightful section.

The river rises near Priory Gardens in Orpington, then passes through St Mary Cray and St Pauls Cray before flowing under Footscray High Street and entering Footscray Meadows. Beyond the Meadows, there is no public access to the river until it reaches The Old Mill at Bexley Village and flows under Bexley High Street. There is further public access in the grounds of Hall Place, and the river then passes through Crayford before joining the River Darent about a mile before that river meets the Thames.

# North Cray

North Cray is also an old village, whose parish has since 1557 included the former village of Ruxley. It was always quite small and compact, located a short distance to the north of North Cray Place and the parish church; several older buildings have survived here, and a village character still remains.

From the Tudor period until after the last war the area around was dominated by the grounds of great estates - Foots Cray Place and North Cray Place (which were combined during the 19th century) to the west and south, and Mount Mascal to the east and north.

The area now resembles a settlement along both sides of a major road. North Cray Road, which runs from the Ruxley roundabout northwards to Bexley Village, did not become a major road until 1968. Beforehand it was a narrow winding country lane, which embraced the present St James Way and the two rural crescents which still survive to the west. The road widening and realignment had some surprising consequences: the lodges of Cray Hall and of Manor Farm became stranded in St James Way on the wrong side of the road, and a medieval hall-house which was directly on the line of the new road was dismantled and re-erected at the Weald and Downland Museum, Singleton, West Sussex.

A few years earlier in 1962 North Cray Place had been demolished for a housing estate. But despite these developments of the 1960s, many old buildings are still there, and the environment on either side of the main road remains obstinately rural. West of the main road are the vast Footscray Meadows around the River Cray, and east of the main road are farmlands and other open space with the great bulk of Joydens Wood and Chalk Wood looming above.

Here one is conscious of being at the very edge of London.

# SIDCUP
## Section 'A'

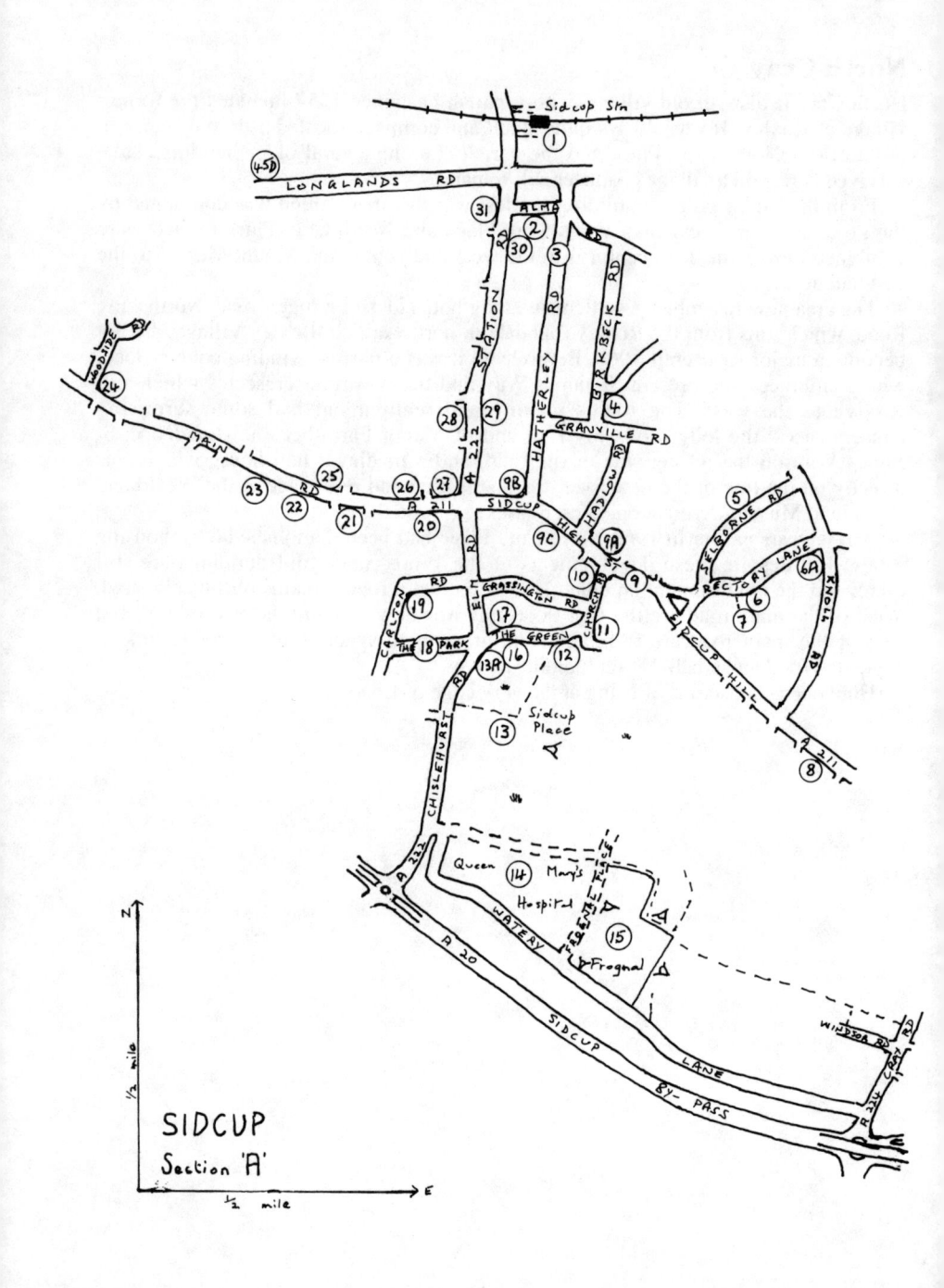

# SIDCUP

## Gazetteer

### Section 'A' CENTRAL SIDCUP

1. **Sidcup Station** has a booking office of 1988 on the south (up) side, which with its steeply gabled glazed entrance is the best designed modern railway building on the Dartford Loop Line. The station was opened in 1866; the platform canopies are of 1937, the footbridge of 1965.

2. **The Alma**, Alma Road. An attractive pub, probably c1866, originally called The Railway Tavern.

3. ***87/95 Hatherley Road**, two pairs and a detached house, and opposite on the east side, the terrace of **nos 66/74 (Alma Villas)**. These two groups c1872 have wild and fantastic ornamentation, nos 87/95 being the more striking. There is a profusion of chevron and dogtooth decoration, and amazing stonework with wonderful detailing of birds and animals, fruit and leaves. Note in particular the square bay of no 91 extending three storeys to a weird pagoda-like rooflet, and the freakish bargeboards of no 95.

4. **Doreen Bird College**, Birkbeck Road. This building of 1882 with its quirky decorative features was originally the **Sidcup National School**. It is now a dance academy and adult education centre.

5. **Selborne Court**, 23 Selborne Road, is a large and impressive classical-style house c1903 with a fine baroque frontispiece.

6. **White Walls**, Rectory Lane, an attractive romantic house c1910 in vaguely Arts & Crafts style.

Further along Rectory Lane is another distinctive house of c1910, **Toucy & Selwood (6A)**, the front rather difficult to see, but the rear, with two full height bows and a profusion of pargetting, readily visible from Knoll Road.

7. ***Old Forge Way**. Nos 1/15 are a delightful enclave of vernacular houses off Rectory Lane, formed by two terraces leading to a semi-circular group. The pattern continues round the corner in Rectory Lane with nos 16/17.

They were designed by Kenneth Dalgleish in 1936 in the style of 17th & 18th century cottages of the Kent & Sussex Weald. The upper floors are tile-hung, weatherboarded or half-timbered, the ground floors red brick. Note the planked front doors, and the rainwater butts.

**8. Ursula Lodges,** Sidcup Hill. A fine group of almshouses built 1972 around a square with a pond; the front entrance is round the corner in Eynswood Drive. They replaced previous buildings funded by the Berens family of Sidcup Place in 1847, and from this time a low brick wall to the east survives.

**9. Sidcup High Street** still follows the winding course.of the old road from London to Maidstone which was improved by the New Cross Turnpike Trust in 1781.

The oldest part is to the east, around ***The Black Horse (9A)**, an old coaching inn with a highly attractive frontage which preserves its basic appearance of the time when the road was improved in 1781.

Further development took place in the late 19th century after the arrival of the railway, and above the modern shopfronts much of the facades and roofline has hardly changed since that time.

In particular note the upper floor of **nos 63/75 (9B)**, of the 1880s, in classical style with some small circular windows. This group adjoins the **Cannon Cinema** at no 77, the only cinema left in the Sidcup or Bexley area; the cinema entrance is c1933, but the actual auditorium is of 1911 and is located behind **Kings Hall**, a building c1870 with patterned brick, Gothic windowheads and other decorative detail.

**No 64 (9C)**, c1881, is the only building in the High Street to retain the appearance of the original house with an unaltered ground floor.

**10. 1/10 Church Road.** This attractive terrace of cottages of 1852 was on the original lane from Sidcup to.Chislehurst. Some have been considerably altered.

**11. Church of St John the Evangelist.** A large, heavy church designed by George Fellowes Prynne in 1901; it incorporates the chancel of an earlier church of 1882. It is of stock brick, with red brick dressings, and is in Gothic style with many lancet windows. Dominating the west front is the squat base of a steeple which was never completed.

Towards the rear on the south wall is a stone recording the laying of the foundations of the first church in 1841.

> The first church on the site was completed in 1844 as a district church in the Parish of Chislehurst, and was later to become Sidcup Parish Church. (Note that columns from the outside arcade of the first church were incorporated in shops at Station Road, *see 31.*) The second church was built in 1882. The present church was completed in 1901, retaining the chancel, lady chapel and churchyard wall from the second church.

The exterior may seem rather uninspired, but the ***interior** is well worth viewing. It is wide and imposing, and has many interesting furnishings (many from the first church, some imported and older).

> *The church is often open, particularly in the mornings; otherwise ask for Mrs Isobel Darby at St Johns Lodge, The Green, opposite, or call at the Vicarage, 13 Church Avenue.*

The dominant feature is the transition from the lofty nave into the older and smaller chancel, eased by splayed sections, covered with tiered figures of apostles and archangels, which flank the chancel arch. Note also the barrel vault of the roof; and the wide arches of the arcade, each with two narrow clerestory windows above.

In the baptistery to the right of the entrance doors is a font of white Carrara marble, with fine carvings. On a nearby pillar is a painting 'The Martyrdom of St Stephen', said to be of the School of Titian c1550.

There is a fine stone chancel screen with wrought iron gates. To the left of the screen is the pulpit, and to the right the lectern; both furnishings are quite splendid. The pulpit is of 1651, very ornately carved Flemish woodwork from Antwerp; note the figures of the four evangelists (the other figure, of a lady, is a later addition), and the two grotesque faces on either side of the steps. The lectern is of 1776, probably Dutch, of brass on a finely carved wooden base.

In the chancel note the oak canopy on twisted columns over the altar, the marble bas-relief of da Vinci's 'The Last Supper', and two finely carved sanctuary chairs, on either side of the altar. The stained glass in the chancel, and in the Lady Chapel alongside, is by Sir Ninian Comper 1952.

The **churchyard** has many tombs and monuments, but note in particular, towards the rear on the right, the curious bronze cross to Mary Sheffield 1899, conspicuous in its blue colour, with strange art nouveau motifs.

**12. *Place Cottage**, The Green. An attractive brick house, with a symmetrical pattern of windows and dormers; it is of late 18th century appearance, but the structure is of a timber-framed house, probably c1675. There are substantial extensions to the rear, and a two storey bay to the east, added c1895.

Adjacent, to the west, are two very fanciful, romantic and richly detailed houses. The larger, **Cluny Cottage**, has an ornate porch and steep bargeboarded gable; the lower floor is of knapped flint, the upper floor jettied and tile-hung. It was originally three cottages of 1886. The smaller, **Summerfield Lodge**, was built in virtually identical style c1986, a hundred years later.

Further west, at the beginning of Sidcup Place, is **Freeby**, a large house in vernacular style with tile-hung upper floor, of 1896.

**13. *Sidcup Place.** An extraordinary building, partly 18th century, but very irregular because of its 19th century extensions. It has a wonderful location, surrounded by a great area of open space.

> From 1822 to 1919 Sidcup Place was owned by the Berens family, who funded the Sidcup National School, Ursula Lodges and (in large part) St Johns Church. It was purchased by the Chislehurst & Sidcup UDC after its formation in 1933, and incorporated their council chamber. It was transferred to the London Borough of Bexley in 1965, and it is now used by the Directorate of Engineering and Works.

The old core, said to date back to 1743, is at the south-east corner; it was originally a square, with bastions projecting at each corner, like a 'star fort'. Of these bastions, only the north-east one now remains free, the south-east and south-west ones having being merged into a later bay facing south; the north-west one disappeared with other 19th century extensions.

The main extensions were of 1853, including the main part of the imposing south front with its two large gables above handsome bay windows, and the short open arcade leading from the north-east bastion. The north front, including the fine tower, with its elegant concave roof, and the gable, below which is the coat of arms of the Berens family, was added probably c1896. Note the mounting-block hard up against the foot of the tower. Projecting from the north front is the stable-block, with the section to the right c1780 and the section to the left substantially altered c1930; and there are modern extensions further west.

Of the **interior**, the reception area is readily accessible. Though it embraces part of the original 1743 building, the grand staircase, fine plaster ceilings and stone fireplace were all added in 1853.

Other rooms of the interior are not normally open to the public. The most interesting are the two rooms of the general office, which are both part of the 1743 building; they contain a fine marble fireplace c1823 - the delicately carved classical figures on the horizontal piece are attributed to John Flaxman, and the two flanking female figures on the vertical pieces are by John Gibson - as well as grotesque masks over the internal arches. Also worth seeing is the old council chamber, in two parts - a room of 1853 with a fine plaster ceiling, and a room of 1924.

*Those with a serious interest in seeing the rooms normally inaccessible to the public should ask at reception, and it may be possible to arrange this.*

To the south is the **rose garden**, the old kitchen garden, still retaining part of its 19th century walling. To the east is a long **ha-ha** of knapped flint; from this area there are excellent views over a vast open space towards the Cray Valley and Joydens Wood beyond.

On Chislehurst Road is **The Red Lodge (13A)**, a red brick building, probably c1896, which was a lodge for Sidcup Place; it is now becoming derelict. It has distinct architectural similarities with the north front of Sidcup Place.

**14. Queen Mary's Hospital.** This postwar complex covers a vast area.

The original hospital was opened in 1917 in the old mansion of Frognal *(see 15)*, and this was followed by a series of temporary buildings further east on what is now waste land. The new hospital was officially opened to the west of Frognal in 1974.

Approaching from Chislehurst Road to the west, first one comes to the Maternity Wing, a functional building of 1966, and then a great building of 1974 in pleasing bands of red brick and glass, comprising the Casualty Wing and the larger Main Block.

Further east, crossing Frognal Place, is the mansion of Frognal *(see below)*, no longer part of the Hospital. To the north of Frognal are the nurses homes, mainly completed 1965, and the Frognal Centre, in the same pleasing style as the Main Block.

**15. \*\*\*Frognal** is the oldest and the most interesting building in Sidcup, but it is the most difficult to view. It is very large, roughly square, with a central courtyard. Its present appearance is predominantly of c1670, and highly attractive, despite a series of later extensions to the west and north. It incorporates timber-framed structure of the 15th and 16th centuries, and the stone foundations are in part 16th century.

There was a house on the site at least by the 13th century. It was acquired by Sir Philip Warwick in the 16th century, and the present main facades were built by his heirs. In 1752 it was purchased by Thomas Townshend, who became Lord Sydney and gave his name to the first European settlement in Australia, and it remained in the Sydney family until 1915.

Frognal was then acquired by the War Office to become a hospital, and it later became a nurses home. In 1980, some years after the new Queen Mary's Hospital had been completed, it was sold. Subsequent owners have carried out some restoration work on the buildings, but at present no future use has been agreed, and the buildings are empty and appear to be becoming derelict.

Hall Place, west range (c1540-60, c1649-60) - *Bexley 1*

The Kings Head (late 16th century, late 19th century) - *Bexley 8*

**Church of St Mary
(early 13th century,
restored Basil Champneys 1883)**
- *Bexley 24*

**Highstreet House (1761)** - *Bexley 23*

The Old Mill (1972) - *Bexley 40*

Faesten Dyke, Joydens Wood (probably 5th century) - *Bexley 82B*

Church of St John the Evangelist (George Low, 1882-90) - *Bexley 52*

Golden Lion (1901) - *Bexleyheath 5*

Christ Church (William Knight, 1877) - *Bexleyheath 11*

Woolwich Building Society (Broadway Malyan, 1989)- *Bexleyheath 22*

**80 Lion Road (possibly 17th century)** - *Bexleyheath 37*

**Royal Oak (present appearance probably 1863)** - *Bexleyheath 39*

The Red House, west range (Philip Webb, 1859) - *Bexleyheath 40*

The Red House, rear view (Philip Webb, 1859) - *Bexleyheath 40*

**Danson Mansion
(Sir Robert Taylor &
Sir William Chambers,
1763-68)-**
*Welling 9*

**Chapel House (c1770) -**

*Welling 10*

**Church of St Mary the Virgin (Thomas Ford, 1955)** - *Welling 16*

**Church of Christ the Saviour (early 13th century)** - *Welling 12*

**89/93 Hatherley Road (c1872)** - *Sidcup 3*

**Summerfield Lodge (c1986) & Cluny Cottage (1886)** - *Sidcup 12*

**Frognal, south range (c1670)** - *Sidcup 15*

**Sidcup Place (1743, 1853, c1896)** - *Sidcup 13*

Manor House (c1790) - *Sidcup 17*

The Woodman (Kenneth Dalgleish, 1931) - *Sidcup 43*

**The Hollies, water tower (Thomas Dinwiddy, c1901)** - *Sidcup 46*

**Lamorbey House, east front (John Shaw, 1837-42)** - *Sidcup 50*

Seven Stars (probably 16th century) - *Footscray 5*

Tudor Cottages (late 15th or early 16th century) - *Footscray 6*

All Saints Church (c1330,
extended & restored by Henry Hakewill c1863) - *Footscray 13*

Five Arch Bridge (1782) - *Footscray 17A*

**Gothic bath-house (c1766) -**
*North Cray 10*

**Loring Hall (c1760)**
*North Cray*

The main facades of c1670 are predominantly red brick, two storey, with long rows of finely proportioned windows. The finest range faces east, the one storey bay to the right being a later extension. The south range is also attractive, despite the additions to the west. Both east and south fronts have fine entrance doorcases. The north and west ranges are partly obscured by later extensions, mainly at the north-west corner; these extensions (partly 18th century, but mainly 19th century) spoil the symmetry of the complex, though they are mostly quite harmoniously designed.

*There is no public access to the building at all. The grounds are surrounded by fencing, wire or walls, and are guarded by a security firm, which employs vicious sounding dogs. There are views from outside the grounds, but these are not very satisfactory, particularly of the south and east fronts. Details of these views are set out below.*

The most accessible view is of the north front, from a car park on Frognal Place. The near view is dominated by 19th century extensions, though part of the c1670 range can be seen beyond. (There is another view of the north front from behind the Frognal Centre.)

As one walks from this car park towards Watery Lane, there is a view of the west front, dominated by the extensions but including part of the c1670 range; this walk also gives a sideways view of the south front.

On Watery Lane is the main gateway, but it is boarded up; however, through a slit in the gate there is a view (though not very satisfactory) of the south range. Just to the east of this entrance is a fine gate c1720, though it is in poor condition; from this point there is in winter another (and better) view of the south range. The red brick walling along the Watery Lane boundary is in part 18th century.

It is particularly frustrating that the east range is the most difficult to see. It can be viewed properly only in winter from a densely overgrown area, where the original temporary buildings of Queen Mary's Hospital were located. In the summer there are only tantalising glimpses of the east range through the great bank of trees and shrubs. This area, which has now become a vast unofficial nature reserve, rather wild and wonderful, can be accessed from Watery Lane, beyond the fencing; from a path which can be followed alongside the fencing behind the Frognal Centre; or from a path leading from the open space to the south of the modern nurses homes.

From Cray Road, further east, a footpath (accessible between Mayfield Villas and no 61, or at the end of Windsor Road) leads to a long avenue of lime trees, which was part of an original approach way to Frognal. At the end of this avenue are the old grounds of the hospital, with the view in winter of the east front mentioned above.

**16. Sidcup Green.** This small tract of common land is separated from the grounds of Sidcup Place by a screen-belt of tall lime trees on a mound. The **War Memorial** commemorates the dead of both world wars.

**17. *Manor House,** The Green. A very handsome house of red brick c1790 in a prominent position opposite Sidcup Green.
It was built on the site of an old farmhouse, and was originally called Place Green House. It was named Manor House in the 1860s, though there never was a manor of Sidcup. It is now used as the Registry Office by Bexley Borough Council.
The house has many attractive features. The central bays of the front project slightly; above the portico of four slender Tuscan columns positioned side by side is a great recessed arch enclosing a Venetian window, and at the top is a dentilled pediment. There are full-height bows at the rear, and on each side. The extension to the right is of the 1930s and sympathetic, and beyond is an early 19th century stable block.

**18. The Park** was a development of the 1870s. Three houses remain from that time - Kingston House on the south side, Westburton and Amberley on the north side. **30 Elm Road,** round the corner, is part of the same development.
 At the corner with Chislehurst Road is an **'anonymous' pillar box,** ie without a royal cypher, a relatively rare type, c1880.

**19. Carlton Road.** The northern arm of this road, with its avenue of plane trees, has on both sides a complete series of imposing though rather sombre pairs, c1880. The houses are impressive as a group, with their gables, large dormers with ornate stonework, and terracotta detailing.

**20. United Services Club,** 108 Main Road, formerly known as Maison Rouge. This is an imposing building, probably c1880, with its Gothic doorway and stepped gables along the frontage.

**21. The Crescent.** A fine semi-circular green with cedar trees. It was once ringed by great late 19th century houses, of which **122 Main Road** c1878 is the only one remaining.

**22. 140 Main Road,** formerly called Adelaide House. A detached house, probably of the 1830s. It is now part of a builders yard, and seems in poor condition.

**23. Sidcup Fire Station,** Main Road. A striking Edwardian classical red brick building of 1914, with great round archways on either side of the entrance. It was built as a combined Fire Station, Council Offices & Council Chamber for Sidcup UDC.

**24. Nursery House,** 231 Main Road, a small building of the 1840s, with a verandah added c1900. Adjacent to the north are **2/8 Woodside Road,** probably of the 1860s.
 This area retains a village atmosphere, and is sometimes called **Longlands,** after an early 18th century mansion which was demolished in 1885; its location was further west where Park Hill Road is now.

**25. Christ Church,** Main Road. A large ragstone church of 1901, rather late for its archetypal Victorian Gothic appearance. Uninspired externally; the ugly corrugated iron shed at the south-east hides the place where preparations for a tower were begun but never carried out. The **interior** *(contact the Vicarage, 16 Christchurch Road, 081-308 0835)* is quite imposing and very Gothic, with a very tall chancel arch.

**26. St Lawrence of Canterbury Church**, Main Road. This large Roman Catholic church is of 1906. It consists of a great central block with gabled projections on each side; note the chequerboard pattern of bricks and stone on the gable facing south. An attractive postwar community centre is attached at the rear.

The **interior** is interesting *(if not already open, contact the Presbytery, 1 Hamilton Road, 081-300 2480)*, and clearly reflects the exterior design; the central area is under a great dome, and there are broad round arches to the projecting chancel, transepts and entrance.

Adjacent to the west is **no 109 (St Lawrences House)**, a large and handsome classical house of 1924. It was originally a school, and is now the house of the Marist Fathers.

**27. Sidcup Police Station,** Main Road. A pleasing red brick building of 1902, enlivened by its stone porch and balcony.

**28. Bexley Music Centre**, 27 Station Road, is an unusual building c1900, formerly a school; it has a rather dramatic corner block with Ionic columns in a recessed porch and a pretty cupola on top.

**29. Sidcup Community Church Centre**, Station Road. A Victorian Gothic church by George Baines of 1888, originally the Congregational Church. It is notable for the profusion of foiled tracery in the windows. The interior has been pleasingly modernised; all the foils have pretty stained glass.

**30. 86a Station Road.** Apart from the modern shopfront, this is a handsome red brick neo-Georgian building of 1911. Note the oriel, and the pediment with a swag.

**31. 75 & 89 Station Road**, two shops originally built c1882, still incorporate columns which were removed from the first parish church of 1844 *(see 11)*, where they formed part of the outside arcade.

# SIDCUP Section 'B'

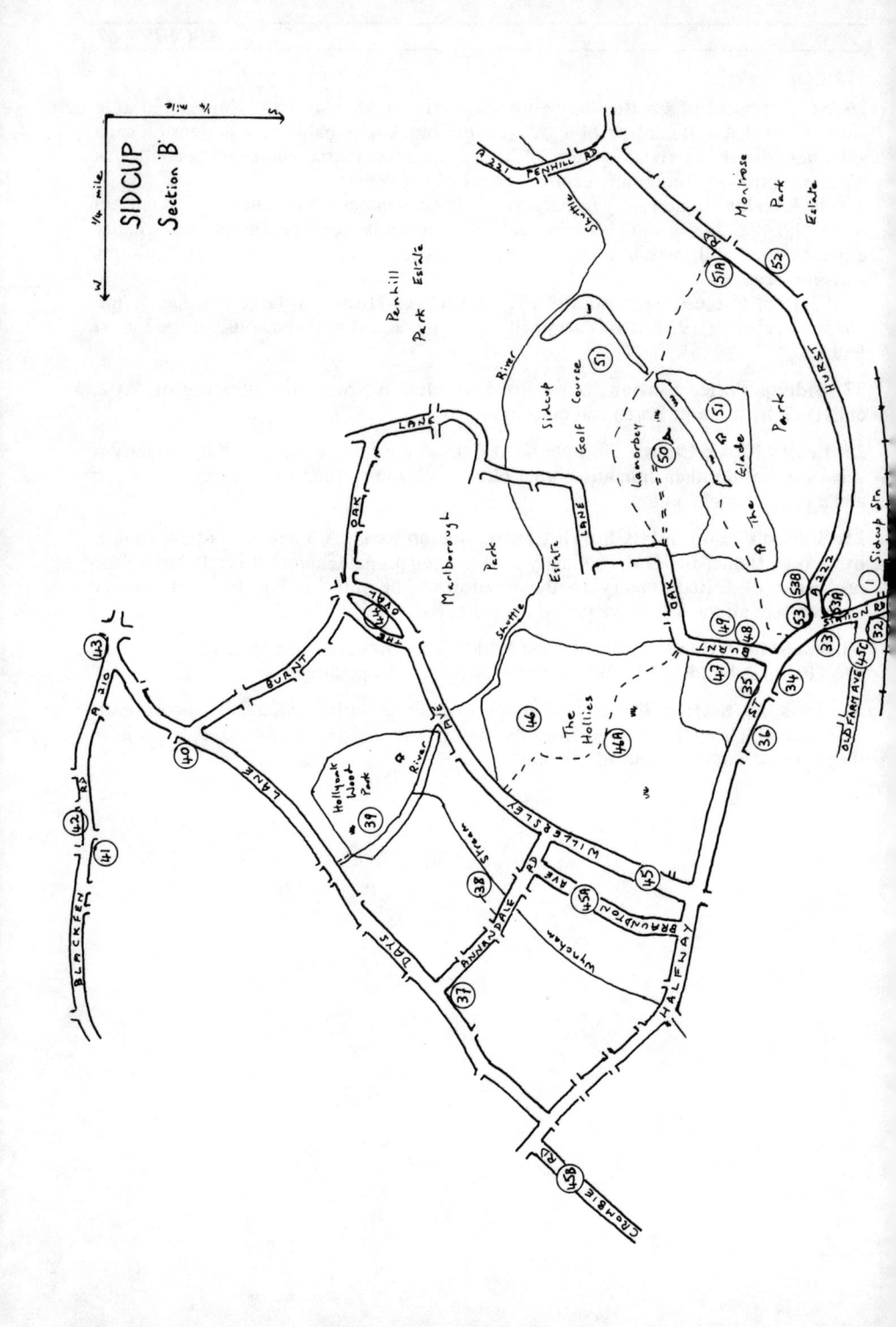

# SIDCUP

## Gazetteer

### Section 'B' LAMORBEY & BLACKFEN

**32. 111 Station Road.** The first shop on the left as you proceed north under the railway bridge is an attractive neo-Georgian building c1933 by Kenneth Dalgleish, with gently bowed windows.

**33. Lamorbey Baths**, Station Road. This is recognisably an old Odeon cinema of 1935, converted in the 1960s. The cream faienced rectangular tiles can still be seen on the adjoining shops on either side.

**34. *21/35 Halfway Street.** A remarkable group of older houses, which formed the nucleus of the old hamlet of Halfway Street; they include two timber-framed houses which are 400-500 years old. From east to west, the group comprises:
   No 21 **(White House)**, c1877.
   No 23 **(Lilac Cottage)**, c1800.
   ***Nos 25/27**, a timber-framed house bearing a Bexley Civic Society plaque with the date 1450. It has been much restored and altered - it was originally one house with a central entrance, the right-hand section being added much later.
   No 29 **(Halfway Cottage)**, probably of the 1830s.
   No 31 **(Fern Cottage)**, probably c1840.
   ***No 33 (Farm Cottage)**, a small timber-framed hall-house, bearing a plaque with the date c1500. From the street it is hidden behind its front garden wall, and behind the adjoining **no 35 (Old Farm)**, though it can be seen that the upper floor is jettied towards the west. The old building incorporated the rear part of no 35, but the main part of no 35 was added much later, probably late 19th century.

**35. 50 Halfway Street.** The right-hand part of this house is 18th century, with a strangely skewed roof; the left-hand part is mid 19th century. The house is being restored as part of a small housing development.

**36. Ye Olde Black Horse**, 43 Halfway Street. A very ornate pub of 1892 with all sorts of decorative features. It was rebuilt on the site of a much older pub; the building bears shields saying 'built 1692' and 'rebuilt 1892'.

**37. Church of the Holy Redeemer**, Days Lane. A small, low-lying church of 1933, set back from the road. The exterior, in a subdued art deco style, with a concrete porch and belfry, does not seem of special interest.

The **interior** however is much more interesting, and is also notable for its use of concrete. *(Contact the Vicarage, 64 Days Lane, 081-300 1508.)* The concrete sanctuary arch leads down into twin concrete ambos (like recesses) which serve as pulpit and lectern, and form the most conspicuous feature of the church. Note also the series of curved concrete ribs which are continued down to the ground as buttresses (pierced to give the impression of flying buttresses) and also form narrow arcades along the aisles. In the sanctuary is a curved concrete altar-rail, and under the piscina a small stone V moulding which is actually Norman from Rochester Cathedral *(see also Bexley 67)*. On the front of the gallery is a small painting, 'The Adoration of the Lamb' by Kenneth Hayes 1986, colourful and very imaginative.

**38. Beverley Wood,** approached by a lane off Annandale Road. A pleasant narrow belt of woodland, alongside the Wyncham Stream.

**39. Hollyoak Wood Park,** Days Lane. The park is mainly grassed, but contains a small pleasant clump of ancient woodland, where the Wyncham Stream joins the River Shuttle. It forms part of the Shuttle Riverway.

**40. Days Lane Baptist Church.** This church of 1966 is imposing and quite jaunty, with long roofs swooping down both sides to end with slightly curled up eaves. Its great gabled east end has a central elongated window stretching from the ground right up to the apex.

**41. Church of the Good Shepherd,** Blackfen Road. A small church of 1965, consisting of a multi-angled copper dome with fleche and glazed sides, on top of a red brick base. The exterior design is unusual, but the interior is quite ordinary, mostly now used as a hall with the church a small section at the east end.

**42. 77/79 Blackfen Road,** an attractive pair c1905, originally farmworkers cottages for Westwood Farm.

**43. The Woodman,** in the heart of the Blackfen shopping centre. An extraordinary pastiche pub by Kenneth Dalgleish 1931, looking like a much older building.

**44. The Oval,** a crescent of mock-Tudor shops, built in 1933. It faces a crescent of the Marlborough Park Estate across an oval of open space, and the whole layout is most attractive. The estate was built by New Ideal Homesteads in the early 1930s *(see Bexley 74)*.

**45. Willersley Avenue.** From Halfway Street up to the junction with Annandale Road is a remarkable sequence of picturesque chalet-style houses of the early 1930s. **Braundton Avenue (45A),** which runs parallel, also has a sequence of such houses.

They are perhaps reminiscent of a New Ideal Homesteads style, but much more imaginative. Great sweeping roofs lead from the top of the ground floor up to a white gable at the apex of each pair. The windows of each floor are topped by red-tiled canopies, and each pair of first floor bowed windows is flanked by porthole windows.

The front gardens have only low front walling, and there are many trees. Willersley Avenue has ample grass verges to the road as well. It all produces a delightful ambience, and there has been limited alteration to the original houses.

There are in fact many fine sequences of houses displaying variations on the chalet style in the area; in particular, note **Crombie Road (45B)** and the eastern end of **Old Farm Avenue (45C)**. Note also, south of the railway line, the series of houses on the northern side of **Longlands Road (45D)**, which, though not in the chalet style, have fine windows, tiled canopies and other ornamental features.

**46. *The Hollies.** This vast area was previously used for children's homes, which were built from 1901 in the grounds of a mid 19th century mansion. It still retains a parkland atmosphere, though it has been in the course of redevelopment for housing since 1990.

> The mansion called The Hollies was built c1853 on the site of a Tudor house, in the centre of a large estate. From 1901 the Greenwich and Deptford Board of Guardians, as an offshoot of the Greenwich Union Workhouse, set up a self-contained village for over 500 children. The workhouse system was abandoned in 1929 and the homes were taken over by the London County Council. In 1965 they were handed over to Southwark Borough Council, who gradually closed the homes down.

In the centre is the mansion of c1853, **The Hollies (46A)**, which became the administrative centre for the homes; it is rather gaunt, in a sort of Jacobean style. Nearby are the old stables, also c1853 and becoming derelict.

To the north are a series of large buildings built c1901 for the Board of Guardians by Thomas Dinwiddy. First is the gymnasium and swimming bath, now converted to a sports centre; and then the steam laundry and boiler house, topped by a massive water tower with four clockfaces, now converted for housing. Beyond, in Acacia Way, are four great three storey blocks - The Beeches, The Firs, The Limes, The Oaks; at the end of Acacia Way is the old infirmary. Other Edwardian blocks can be seen all around. .

The redevelopment is a mixture of new houses and refurbished Edwardian buildings, with much open space retained and in parts quite attractive. The main entrance to the complex is in Burnt Oak Lane, where there is an Edwardian lodge, and there are other entrances from Willersley Avenue.

**47. Burnt Oak School**, a large and powerful red brick.building. It was built for The Hollies 1903-09.

**48. 8 Burnt Oak Lane.** This small house of 1841 was the original **Lamorbey National School**. It remained as a school until 1880. Note the old pinnacle from Lamorbey Chapel c1840 *(see 53)* in the garden to the right.

The adjacent **10/16 Burnt Oak Lane** may look like one large house, with its great bargeboarded gabled centre; it is actually four old cottages, with rustic timber porches each covering two entrances, built for workers on the Lamorbey Estate. A plaque reads 'J.M. 1874' - John Malcolm owned Lamorbey House at the time.

**49. Holy Trinity School**, Burnt Oak Lane, set well back from the road. An amazing building of 1969 by Oliver Steer; with four glazed gables in the centre zigzagging right down to the ground - it 'has to be seen to be believed' (Pevsner).

**50. *Lamorbey House.** A large mansion, now used by the Rose Bruford School of Speech & Drama and by Lamorbey Adult Education Centre. It has a magnificent location in the middle of Lamorbey Park *(see 51)*, the south front looking down towards the picturesque lake.

The first substantial house on the site was built c1515. This house was rebuilt 1744-48 by William Steele (a director of the East India Company), and substantial additions and improvements were made by Dr David Orme (a West Indian trader) c1784. From 1812 to 1910 the estate belonged to the Malcolm family *(see also 48, 53)*, also West Indian traders, who transformed the external appearance of the house.

The house became a hotel in 1910 (it is described in Ursula Bloom's book 'A Roof and Four Walls'), and part of the estate was leased to Sidcup Golf Club and in due course parts sold to New Ideal Homesteads. In 1946 it was acquired by the Kent Education Committee, and four schools were eventually opened on the estate. The house and the park are now owned by the London Borough of Bexley.

*The grounds of Lamorbey House are normally open to the public, allowing views of the exterior. (Note that archery is often practised in the grounds.) The road entrance is from Burnt Oak Lane; there is also a pedestrian entrance from Hurst Road, involving a long walk through Lamorbey Park.*

The remains of the 18th century building (of 1744-48, altered c1784) are around the north entrance, and around an inner courtyard between two wings to the west; the courtyard cannot readily be seen from outside.

The main, very bulky front facing east and the front facing south were transformed in Jacobean style by John Shaw 1837-42. The east front, in particular, is quite extraordinary. Note the openwork crestings leading up to slender pinnacles on top of the two projecting bays; the strapwork panels include the coats of arms of former owners. Similar crestings, not quite so elaborate, are on the south side. Note also the ornamental posts leading to the east terrace.

*Because most rooms are often in use, the interior is not generally open to the public; however, it is worth ringing 081-300 3024 to make an arrangement with one of the caretakers, who are normally happy to show visitors around at convenient times.*

The most interesting rooms in the **\*interior** are c1840, and are best approached from the south entrance. On the right is the **library**, with an excellent Jacobean-style carved wooden chimneypiece, lovely wooden panelling all around, and fine ceiling plasterwork; and on the left, the **music room**, with a fine carved fireplace with a lion's head. A passage to the left leads to the inner courtyard with the older wings *(see above)*; on the left is the orangery, now the **art room**, with an enormous and fantastic wooden pendant surrounded by smaller pendants, and coved glazing making it look like a conservatory. The grand wooden staircase with its slender twisted banisters is late 18th century; off the landing at the top, a staff toilet has original Japanese-motif wallpaper c1850.

To the north of the house are some interesting outbuildings. Coming along the driveway from Burnt Oak Lane, to the left is the Barn Theatre, modern but using part of the walls and sloping roof of an old barn dating back at least to the mid 19th century. Beyond this is the **coach-house** (with a cupola on top) and adjoining stables, probably c1790. By the car park, behind a 19th century **piggery**, is a pair of old **gardeners cottages**, probably of the 1830s.

The footway from the car park to the north entrance of the house is flanked by outbuildings. Those to the right are more substantial, probably of 1784; though the brought forward section adjoining the house is of 1991. The diminutive one-storey building with a wide Gothic window was a **dairy**, c1840.

Part of an old wall of the kitchen garden, probably of the 1840s, can be seen in The Glade *(see below)*.

**51. Lamorbey Park** contains Lamorbey House *(see above)* and its grounds; a picturesque ornamental lake with two arms; The Glade, a public park; four schools; and the Sidcup Golf Club course. The Glade and (normally) the grounds of Lamorbey House are open to the public, and a public footpath runs right through the Park.
   The footpath runs from the main entrance in Burnt Oak Lane to the entrance in Hurst Road. At first it runs between wire fences, separating the grounds of Lamorbey House from Sidcup Golf Course, to a bridge over a weir between the two arms of the lake; it then passes between the grounds of two schools.
   The western arm of the lake has the grounds of Lamorbey House to the north and The Glade to the south, so there is normally full public access; the eastern arm is entirely within the golf course, and there is no public access. There are footings of an old bath-house c1780 (just visible to the left of the public footpath) by the weir between the two arms. The lake is fed by the River Shuttle, which runs to the north.
   ***The Glade** leads from its entrance in Halfway Street to the southern bank of the lake, providing a fine view of Lamorbey House. It is an attractive park, with fine trees including a ten-trunked cypress near the entrance. It embraces part of an old kitchen-garden wall of the House, probably of the 1840s.
   At the Hurst Road entrance to the Park is **The Lodge (51A)**, 189 Hurst Road, c1860 though altered; it has a jettied half-timbered upper floor with fanciful gables and bargeboards.

**52. Montrose Club**, 158 Hurst Road, formerly known as **Abbeyhill**. An attractive stuccoed building c1830, with later extensions on both sides. From 1862 to 1904 it was the vicarage for Lamorbey Chapel and subsequently Holy Trinity Church.
   It is now surrounded by the **Montrose Park Estate**, built by New Ideal Homesteads *(see Bexley 74)* in the 1930s.

**53. Holy Trinity Church.** A Victorian Gothic ragstone church by Ewan Christian of 1879. The north aisle was added in line with Christian's plan in 1909. It looks very much a rather squat Gothic village church. Timber porch and lychgate.
>   The first Anglican church in Lamorbey was a Chapel (to the parish church of Bexley), built 1840 on a site between the present church and Burnt Oak Lane. It was funded by John Malcolm, who occupied Lamorbey House at the time; in 1862 he bought Abbeyhill *(see 52)* as a vicarage. In 1841 he also funded the first church school, now 8 Burnt Oak Lane *(see 48)*; a pinnacle from the chapel has been preserved in the garden.
>   With the increasing population after the coming of the railway in 1866 it was decided to build a new church, again largely funded by John Malcolm; this became Lamorbey Parish Church. The architect was Ewan Christian; it opened in 1879, though the north aisle was not built until after his death, and his planned tower was never built. It was substantially rebuilt as a replica following war damage.

The ***interior** *(contact the Vicarage, 1 Hurst Road, 081-300 8231)* is wide and low, and attractive; the east window has interesting and imaginative postwar stained glass designed by Martin Travers.
   **Holy Trinity Church Hall (53A)**, Hurst Road. An amazing, rather fanciful long building of 1880; its steeply pitched roof has a narrow pinnacle and great tile-hung gables. It was originally the Lamorbey National School, replacing the school of 1841 *(see 48)* in Burnt Oak Lane. In 1969 it became the Church Hall, after a new school *(see 49)* had been built in Burnt Oak Lane.
   **Universal House (53B)**, 3 Hurst Road. This large neo-Georgian house of 1904 with its prominent dormer windows was a former Vicarage.

# SIDCUP

## Suggested Walks

*It is recommended that the two suggested walks be followed in conjunction with the Gazetteer and the maps, and that the Gazetteer be consulted at each location for a detailed description (all places in bold type are mentioned in the Gazetteer). The first walk covers most locations described in Section 'A'; other locations have not been included, as they might add too much to the length of the walk. The second walk covers all locations in Section 'B' which are in the Lamorbey area; locations in the Blackfen area are not included as they are too thinly spread over quite a large area. Both walks begin and end at Sidcup Station. They follow a more or less circular route, so can be joined at any location.*

**WALK No 1** (including Sidcup High Street, Sidcup Place, Frognal, and Station Road.) Distance approx three miles.

*NB. Note the arrangements in the gazetteer for viewing the interiors of St Johns Church and St Lawrence of Canterbury Church.*

On leaving **Sidcup Station (1)**, turn left along Station Road and left along Alma Road, noting **The Alma (2)** pub on the right. Turn right up **Hatherley Road**, noting **nos 66/74** on the left and **nos 87/95 (3)** on the right. Continue up to the junction with **Sidcup High Street (9)** and turn right, noting **nos 63/75**, the **Cannon Cinema & Kings Hall (9B)** on the right.

Return along the High Street, passing Hatherley Road and noting **no 64 (9C)** opposite, until you reach **The Black Horse (9A)**. Cross the road and proceed along **Church Road**, noting **nos 1/10 (10)** on the right, until you come to the **Church of St John the Evangelist (11)**; try to see the interior, and look in the **churchyard** for the Mary Sheffield cross.

Cross the road to **Place Cottage (12)**, then continue past **Summerfield Lodge & Cluny Cottage (12)**, then bear left past **Freeby** to **Sidcup Place (13)**. Note the ha-ha to the east, then cross the open space diagonally to Frognal Place at the eastern end of the **Queen Mary's Hospital (14)** buildings. From here there are views of the north and west ranges and, from Watery Lane beyond, of the south range of **Frognal (15)** - *see the gazetteer for details.*

Return along the approach drive past the Hospital buildings to Chislehurst Road and turn right. Continue until you reach **The Red Lodge (13A)** on the right; just beyond note **Sidcup Green (16)** and **Manor House (17)**. Cross Chislehurst Road, which becomes Elm Road at this point, to **The Park (18)**; walk to the end and turn right into **Carlton Road (19)**, bearing right until you are back in Elm Road, then turn left. Continue to the crossroads, then turn left onto Main Road.

74

Note the **United Services Club (20)** and **The Crescent (21)**, then cross the road to **Christ Church (25)**. Return along Main Road, passing **no 109** and **St Lawrence of Canterbury Church (26)** (try to see the interior), until you reach **Sidcup Police Station (27)** at the crossroads. Turn left down **Station Road**, passing **Bexley Music Centre (28)** on the left and **Sidcup Community Church Centre (29)** on the right. Much further down, note **no 86a (30)** on the right and continue until you are back at the railway bridge and Sidcup Station.

**WALK No 2** (including Halfway Street, Lamorbey Park and Lamorbey House). Distance approx three miles.

*It is worth making advance arrangements - see the gazetteer - to view the interiors of Lamorbey House and Holy Trinity Church.*

On leaving **Sidcup Station (1)**, turn right up Station Road, and immediately note **no 111 (32)** on the left. Continue on the left side of the road, passing **Lamorbey Baths (33)** until you reach the remarkable group of houses, **21/35 Halfway Street (34)**. Continue along Halfway Street, passing **Ye Olde Black Horse (36)**, until you are opposite Willersley Avenue. Cross the road, proceed up **Willersley Avenue (45)** for a short way, then return to Halfway Street and turn left.

Pass **50 Halfway Street (35)** and turn left up **Burnt Oak Lane**. Note **no 8 & nos 10/16 (48)** and **Holy Trinity School (49)** on the right side of the road, and **Burnt Oak School (47)** on the left side. Continue to the point where Burnt Oak Lane sweeps round to the right; a road bears left into **The Hollies (46)** (if you have time, look at the Victorian mansion and the Edwardian buildings in the centre of the site).

Continue along Burnt Oak Lane and bear right into **Lamorbey Park (51)**. Walk along the driveway to the right which leads to the Rose Bruford School at **Lamorbey House (50)**, passing the **coach-house**, and look round the exterior; try to see the interior. Return to the beginning of the driveway, and turn right along the public footpath which runs initially between wire fences. Continue along the footpath through Lamorbey Park until you eventually reach **The Lodge (51A)**, at the junction with Hurst Road.

Turn right along Hurst Road, passing the **Montrose Club (52)** on the left, and continue for some distance until you come to **Holy Trinity Church (53)**; try to see the interior. Note **Holy Trinity Church Hall (53A)** opposite. Turn left down Station Road, and you are quickly back at Sidcup Station.

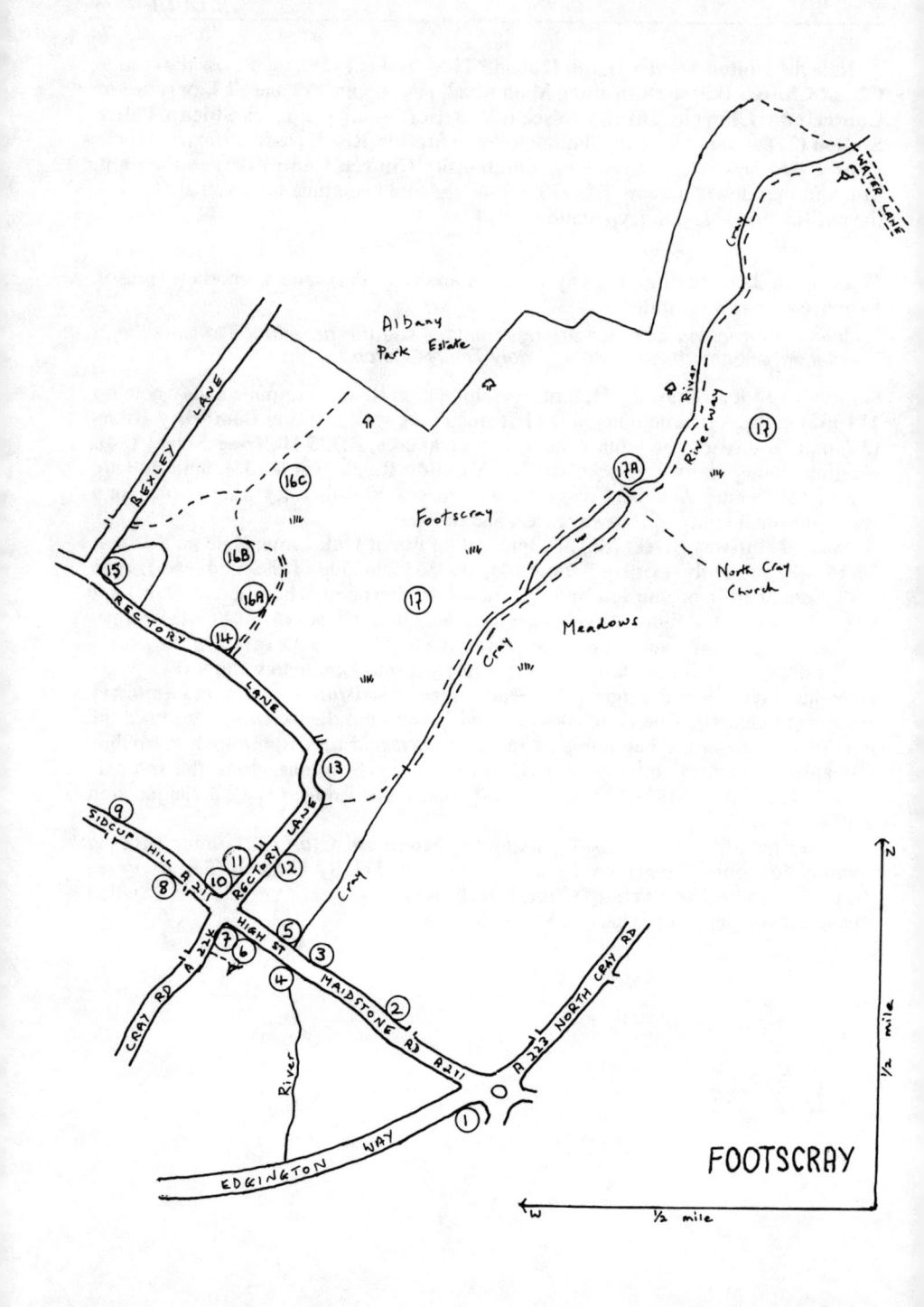

# FOOTSCRAY

# FOOTSCRAY

## Gazetteer

**1. Richard Klinger works,** Edgington Way. A large factory of 1936 by Wallis Gilbert & Partners, considered to be influenced by Dutch Expressionism. The frontage is symmetrical and impressive, with long horizontal bands of brown brick and glass, and similar but vertical bands of brick and glass in the central tower.

**2. 65/79 Maidstone Road.** A fantastic mock-Tudor shopping parade c1930, with oriel windows, curved eaves, Tudor chimneys, and a steep and narrow half-timbered central gable.

**3. *Sidcup Technology Centre,** Maidstone Road. A long striking building of 1985 designed by GMW. It has great bands of glass and baked white aluminium sheeting, with the first floor suspended on pilotis, and three circular brick staircase towers.

The western range arches over the River Cray, on the site of the old papermill which was demolished in 1929; it is a picturesque setting with a weir and the old mill-pond - there are views from the front lawn of the Technology Centre, as well as from the garden and car park behind the Seven Stars pub.

**4. Footscray Bridge.** The south side of the road bridge retains its brick wall c1815, and the wall with the old spans and breakwater can be seen from the modern footbridge alongside. The bridge was widened in 1909.

**5. *Seven Stars,** Footscray High Street. The weatherboarded range at right angles to the road, with its great gable end taking up virtually the whole pavement, is 16th century, though the windows and the stuccoed base are 19th century. The range at right angles, parallel with the road, was added in 1912.

The **interior** is attractive; above a fireplace is a carving of a madonna's head surrounded by seven stars - this is an old stone which was found in a well on the site. The garden behind overlooks the River Cray and the site of the old papermill.

**6. *Tudor Cottages,** Footscray High Street. This timber-framed building with its jettied upper floor was originally a late 15th or early 16th century hall-house. It was completely restored in 1974, when the bay with projecting window to the right was added. It has been virtually rebuilt behind the facade, and is now used as offices.

Go along Evry Road and into the car park at the rear to see, adjoining a long rear modern extension, an attractively restored section of the original building.

**7. The Red Lion,** Footscray High Street. This pub, which dates back at least to 1823, was largely rebuilt c1936.

To the left is **Prospect House**, a pleasing modern building c1980, which has a jettied upper floor in sympathy with the adjacent Tudor Cottages. It is linked to the Red Lion by a surviving section of a 16th century building.

To the right is **Nexus House**, an attractive building by Campbell Ross 1982, enhancing the village scene as it rounds the corner of Footscray High Street and Cray Road. Like Prospect House, it too has a sympathetic jettied first floor.

**8. Walnut Tree Cottage,** 164 Sidcup Hill, is basically a timber-framed house (see the east side) c1550; it was however refaced c1930, and there is a modern porch.

Immediately to the east are **Ivy Cottages** of 1891 and **170/2 Sidcup Hill** of 1890. On the front of the latter note the initials RAV (Robert Arnold Vansittart, who owned Foots Cray Place and North Cray Place at the time).

**9. Footscray Baptist Church**, Sidcup Hill, is dominated by its large Gothic facade of 1885. The first chapel on the site was built 1836, and amongst the profusion of monuments and tombstones in front, some pre-date 1885.

**10. *180/8 Rectory Lane**, known as Belgrave Place. An imposing and highly attractive early Georgian tall red brick terrace. A brick is inscribed 1737, but the terrace is considered to have been built c1760. The rear is weatherboarded. Note the dormers, and the wooden cornice under the roof.

**11. *The Old House,** 170 Rectory Lane. A picturesque house c1820, which may contain some Tudor structure. To the left is a contemporary timber stable block, with a section of old red brick walling in front.

**12. Harenc School**, Rectory Lane. A very quirky long building of 1882 with a low sweeping tile-hung roof, interrupted by three gables and an amazing tall clock tower with a pyramid top. The inscription under the clock reads: 'While ye have light believe in the light that ye may be the children of light'. It was originally the **Footscray National School**; the first school on the site was built in 1816.

**13. *All Saints Church,** Rectory Lane. A small church, the original parish church of Footscray, picturesquely sited by Footscray Meadows. It is basically c1330, but was transformed by alterations and restoration by Henry Hakewill c1863. Despite the 19th century rebuilding, it still looks like a rural church many centuries older.

The medieval church had a shorter nave, stretching only as far as the tower at its west end, the chantry chapel alongside to the north under its parallel roof, and a shorter chancel.

The alterations of c1863 included the extension beyond the tower to the west; the tower, which is wooden with a shingled spire, was retained in position (though rebuilt as a replica c1901) and so is now over a central part of the nave. Also, a new roof was provided, and much of the exterior was faced with flint. The west porch and doorcase are c1500, and the door itself c1650; they were reset in their present position in the c1863 alterations.

In 1872, the chancel was extended a short distance to the east. The vestry to the east of the chantry chapel is of 1973.

Two windows on the south side of the nave at the east end, and the four chantry chapel windows to the north remain from the 14th century church; these windows can be distinguished by their trefoil heads. All other windows are 19th century or later.

The *interior has lots of interesting features, and is well worth viewing *(contact The Rectory, Rectory Lane, phone 081-300 7096)*. Apart from the six windows mentioned above, remaining from the medieval church are: the very wide arch to the chantry chapel, the Norman font, and the Lady de Vaughan monument.

On entering the church from the west porch, the font is situated immediately to the right; it is of Purbeck marble, c1190, and is probably from an earlier church on the site. On either side of the nave walls at this point are large paintings of Moses and of Aaron, carried out 1709 as part of an altarpiece.

The open timbered roof of the nave dates from the c1863 rebuilding. There are also some nice Victorian decorations and inscriptions; all the windows have Victorian stained glass.

To the left of the nave, through the wide arch, is the chantry chapel. The monument is under a low Tudor brick arch set in the north wall. It is the remains of the recumbent effigy of Lady de Vaughan, c1350; alongside is the loose head of a chain-mailed knight. The four trefoil-headed windows are 14th century. The painted ceiling is Victorian.

At the east end of the nave, projecting from the south wall beyond the two trefoil-headed windows, is the gate to the rood-loft stairs, dated 1638. Sited under a low Tudor arch, it now leads to the pulpit, which is alabaster and of 1886. In front of the pulpit, a 15th century roodscreen panel has been incorporated into the front of the prayer desk.

In the chancel, the painted ceiling and the reredos are of 1872, the choir stalls & chancel screen c1901.

The **churchyard** has considerable atmosphere. Note in particular, outside the south-east corner of the church, the iron grave slab (a very unusual feature outside the Kent Weald) to Francis Manning 1696. The most prominent tomb is behind the church, to Sir John Pender 1890, a pioneer of the transatlantic cable and former resident of Foots Cray Place. Note also the rustic lych-gate of 1877 at the southern end of the churchyard.

**14. Rokesle**, Rectory Lane. A substantial building, probably basically c1790 though much altered. It was the rectory until the present rectory was built next door c1952.

**15. Dower House Lodge**, a low whitewashed lodge bearing the date 1820. It was the lodge for **Dower House**, a stuccoed mansion c1800, which can be glimpsed through the trees from Rectory Lane and Bexley Lane in the winter; however, it is not visible in the summer, and there is no public access to any point from which it can be viewed.

**16. Foots Cray Place (remains).** The Palladian mansion was burnt down in 1949, but its site can be detected and two interesting outbuildings remain, the Stable Block of c1756 and the Bowls Pavilion of 1903.

Foots Cray Place was built c1754, probably by Isaac Ware, for Bourchier Cleeve, a London pewterer and writer on finance; it was largely modelled on Palladio's Villa Rotonda at Vicenza. In 1822 the estate was bought by Sir Nicholas Vansittart, then Chancellor of the Exchequer, later to become Lord Bexley. He also bought the adjoining North Cray Place in 1833, and the two combined estates remained in the ownership of the Vansittart family until the 1890s, when they were divided once more.

From then until the 1930s Foots Cray Place (though not North Cray Place) was occupied by Lord Waring, of Waring & Gillow, who commissioned Thomas Mawson to undertake a major landscaping of the grounds in 1903. It was bought by Kent Education Committee in 1946 to become a museum, but it was burnt down in 1949. The estate was transferred to the London Borough of Bexley in 1965.

The best approach to the outbuildings and other remains is by a lane leading north from Rectory Lane, just east of Rokesle. First one comes to a long range of red brick **garden wall,** partly 18th century.

Alongside is the **Bowls Pavilion (16A),** designed in 1903 by Frank Atkinson for Lord Waring. At present derelict, it is soon to be restored. It is an extraordinary building, with its dome-shaped roof; behind, to the north, is the bowling green, at present very overgrown.

Beyond one reaches the very handsome red brick *Stable Block (16B),** c1756, with its cupola on top; this is the only building remaining from the original Foots Cray Place. Alongside is a one-storey red brick building c1903, which was the chauffeur's cottage.

On the other side of the Stable Block, to the west, are very elegant 18th century iron **gates,** flanked by red brick gate piers; these lead to the Dutch garden and beyond to the kitchen garden. The Dutch garden has an ornamental pool which was once a fountain. Both gardens are now overgrown; they were laid out by Thomas Mawson, but are still surrounded by garden walls which are partly 18th century. (Visitors with a special interest in seeing these gardens should call at the office in the Stable Block, and it may be possible to arrange this.)

Follow the pathway in front of the Stable Block, bearing round to the right. In a glade to the right are the stone footings of a circular garden structure, which was the base of a fountain. The flat grassed area beyond this is the actual **site of Foots Cray Place (16C).** From this area, terraces lead down to another flat grassed area backed by a yew hedge; these features remain from the formal landscape garden created by Thomas Mawson c1902. Remains of the stonework and bricks can be found in the bushes around.

Further along the pathway is an early 20th century red brick gate pier; eventually the path comes out at Maylands Drive, Albany Park.

17. **\*Footscray Meadows.** An extensive and beautiful area of open space, consisting of parkland, fields, copses and woodland, with some magnificent trees. It embraces the old grounds of both Foots Cray Place and North Cray Place; these were in fact combined for most of the 19th century.

The River Cray runs through the area from south to north. The grounds of Foots Cray Place occupied the southern part of the Meadows to the west of the river, whilst the grounds of North Cray Place occupied the Meadows to the east of the river as well as the remaining area to the west. Capability Brown was involved in the landscaping of the grounds of North Cray Place, of which the most prominent feature is the:

**\*Five Arch Bridge (17A)**. This is a very handsome brick bridge with splayed ends, of 1782, though much rebuilt. It is sited over a weir on the river, and the area all around is picturesque.

On the west side of the river a double avenue of lime trees leads back towards a screen of yew trees; beyond this is the site of Foots Cray Place and its formal garden, and the remaining outbuildings *(see 16)*.

On the east side of the river, around St James Church, are walls and gates from North Cray Place *(see North Cray 3)*.

The meadows have many species of rare waterfowl and other birds. But most unusual is a colony of parakeets, which escaped from captivity c1960 and have since bred successfully here. The areas by the river contain a number of plants very rare in the London area.

The **Cray Riverway** starts to the south of All Saints Church and continues through the Meadows along the east bank of the river (though the walk along the west bank is perhaps more pleasant). One then reaches a section where the river broadens out to form a long, narrow lake; this was created by damming the river with a weir under the Five Arch Bridge, which is reached after about half a mile.

The Riverway continues for a further half mile along the east bank to a modern wooden bridge across the river; this is at the end of Water Lane, and the rear of Loring Hall *(see North Cray 8)* is visible here.

There is a path from the Five Arch Bridge along the west bank, but it is narrow, obstructed by branches in places, and can become very muddy; however, it does pass through a very attractive belt of woodland known as **The Alders**.

Further west is an extensive and quite dense belt of woodland, **North Cray Wood**, beyond which is the Albany Park Estate.

# FOOTSCRAY

## Suggested Walk

*It is recommended that the suggested walk be followed in conjunction with the Gazetteer and the map, and that the Gazetteer be consulted at each location for a detailed description (all places in bold type are mentioned in the Gazetteer). The walk covers most locations described in the Gazetteer; other locations have not been included, as they might add too much to the length of the walk. The walk begins and ends at the Sidcup Technology Centre, Maidstone Road.*
*Try to make an advance arrangement - see the gazetteer - to see the interior of All Saints Church. Distance approx two miles.*

From the **Sidcup Technology Centre (3)**, proceed westwards across **Footscray Bridge (4)** and along Footscray High Street, keeping to the left-hand side of the road. You quickly come to **Tudor Cottages (6)**, and next door **Prospect House, The Red Lion** and **Nexus House (7)**. Cross Cray Road at the crossroads, and continue along Sidcup Hill to **Walnut Tree Cottage (8)**, passing **nos 170/2** and **Ivy Cottages**.

Cross the road and return to the crossroads on the other side, then turn left along **Rectory Lane**. Note **nos 180/8 (10)** and **The Old House (11)** immediately on the left, then **Harenc School (12)** on the right. Continue to **All Saints Church (13)**; try to see the interior, and look at the **churchyard**.

Go through the gateway beyond the Church into **Footscray Meadows (17)**, and bear right towards the river. Follow the west bank of the river up to the **Five Arch Bridge (17A)**. If you have time, leave the river before reaching the bridge and follow the double avenue of lime trees up to see the remains of **Foots Cray Place (16)**.

Cross the bridge and return along the east bank of the river. (If you have time, follow the path straight ahead eastwards from the bridge, leading up to **St James Church** - *see North Cray 3* - but make an advance arrangement to see the interior.)

The path, part of the Cray Riverway, eventually leads out to Rectory Lane beyond All Saints churchyard. Continue to the crossroads, and turn left along Footscray High Street. In a short while you come to the **Seven Stars** pub **(5)**; go into the garden at the rear for the view of the old mill-pond and weir. Cross the bridge, and you are back at the Sidcup Technology Centre.

# NORTH CRAY

## Gazetteer

**1. 77 St James Way** was originally a lodge for Cray Hall *(see 20)*, but was separated from it when North Cray Road was widened and realigned in 1968. It is basically a Victorian Gothick cottage orné, probably c1830, but now double its original size.

Note also, on the corner of St James Way and High Beeches, **68 St James Way (1A)**, a nice cottage of 1891 bearing the initials RAV (Robert Arnold Vansittart, who owned Foots Cray Place and North Cray Place at the time).

**2. 1 St James Way**, a small weatherboarded cottage, probably mid 19th century. It was originally a lodge (though much altered) for Manor Farm, but was separated from it when North Cray Road was widened and realigned in 1968.

Manor Farm, on the opposite side of North Cray Road, is also 19th century, but it is some way back from the road and cannot be seen properly from any point to which the public has access.

**3. St James Church.** This Victorian Gothic ragstone church is of 1852, when the previous church was rebuilt by Edwin Nash. The chancel was extended in 1872. The church is approached along a short lane from North Cray Road, by the junction with St James Way; it is located just north of the site of North Cray Place.

> The earliest reference to a church at North Cray is 1120. In 1557 the parish of North Cray was united with the parish of Ruxley, after Ruxley Church *(see 23B)* was closed.
> In 1822 a Tudor mansion was rebuilt as North Cray Place *(see also Footscray 16)*, and members of the Vansittart family lived there at different periods between 1833 and 1911. It was demolished in 1962, and a housing estate (North Cray Estate, around The Grove) was built on the site. Some walls and a gate remain by the church; the grounds were originally laid out by Capability Brown, and now form part of Footscray Meadows *(see Footscray 17)*.

The main feature of the exterior is the steeple of 1856, with its attractive shingled spire; but note also the east window of 1952, with its strange pattern of three broad lights separated by two narrow lights.

The ***interior*** is well worth viewing *(contact the Rectory, 2 St James Way, 081-300 1655, or Mr Wolwebber, 26 Parsonage Lane, 081-302 2274)*, particularly for the beautifully carved woodwork in the chancel, much of it foreign and considerably older than the church, and for other older furnishings.

The most impressive stained glass is in the east window of 1952, representing Christ surrounded by the Apostles. Other stained glass windows are at the west end, of 1852; at the east end of the north aisle, of 1953; and, more interesting, at the east end of the south aisle, also of 1953, showing the church, St James, and the Five Arch Bridge in Footscray Meadows. The small plain windows along the aisle walls have 16th century stained glass panels inserted.

83

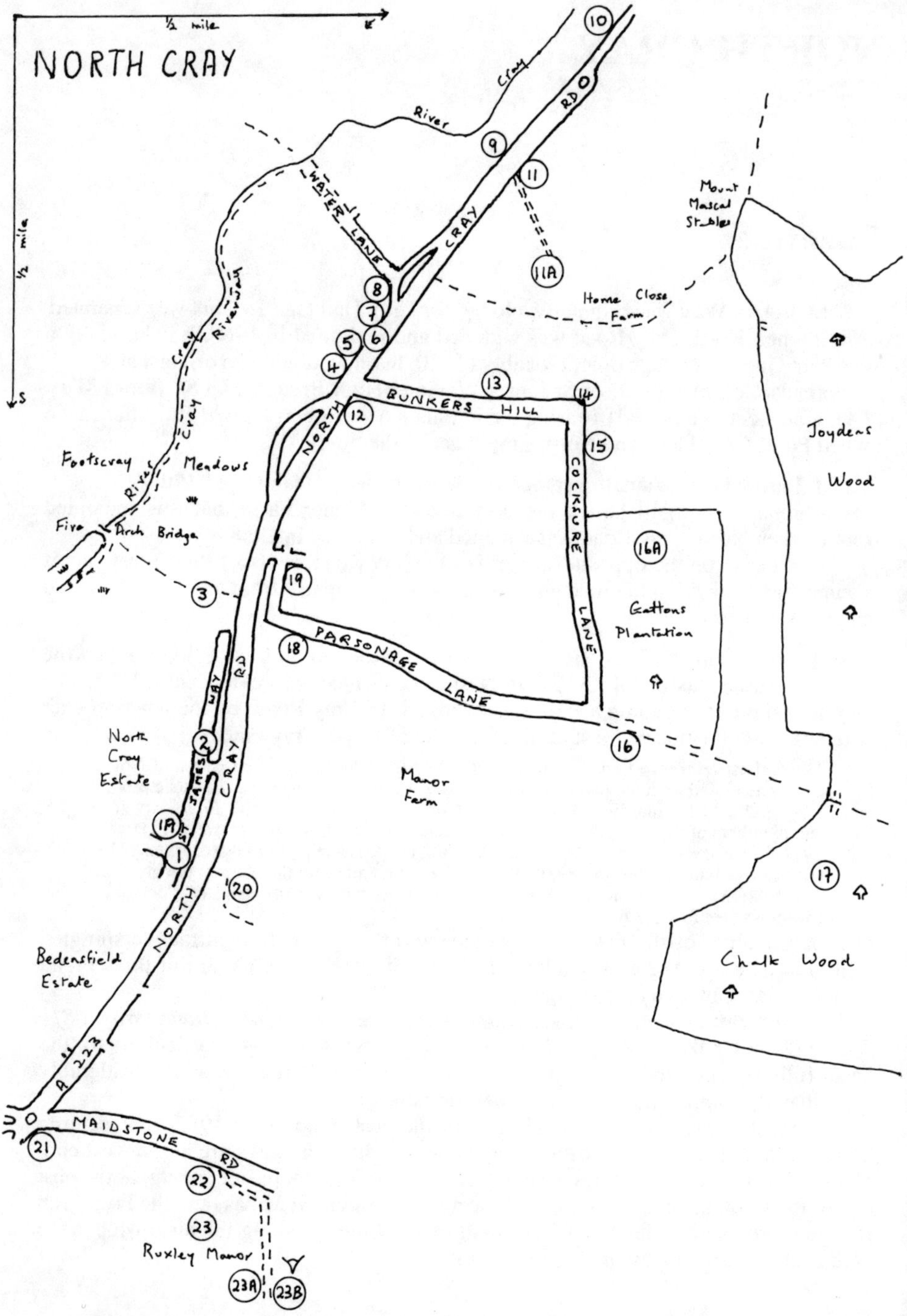

NORTH CRAY
½ mile
½ mile
N
S
River Cray
RD
CRAY
WATER LANE
Mount Mascal Stables
Home Close Farm
Cray Riverway
River Cray
BUNKERS HILL
NORTH
Footscray Meadows
Five Arch Bridge
COCKSURE LANE
Joydens Wood
Gattons Plantation
PARSONAGE LANE
WAY
RD
North Cray Estate
ST JAMES
CRAY
Manor Farm
NORTH
Chalk Wood
Bedensfield Estate
A 223
MAIDSTONE RD
Ruxley Manor
1
1A
2
3
4
5
6
7
8
9
10
11
11A
12
13
14
15
16
16A
17
18
19
20
21
22
23
23A
23B

The carved woodwork in the chancel is so abundant and lavish that it makes a 'unified whole of some splendour' (Pevsner). The woodwork includes: on the front of the stalls, reliefs of Nativity scenes and ornamental foliage panels; behind the stalls to the north, a 15th century relief with attractive small carvings of the Seven Acts of Mercy, flanked by later end panels with Renaissance shellhoods; and, forming a climax, the reredos, which is 15th or 16th century Flemish, with large panels in very bold relief of the Adoration of the Magi and the Flight into Egypt.

Also in the chancel, on the south wall, note the pretty multi-cusped arch to the organ recess, and alongside, the monument to Alice Morris 1894, a magnificent relief by Nelson MacBean of a woman in Grecian draperies with upraised arms. Beneath this is a tablet to Josias Bull 'ye painfulle pastor of the parish' 1656.

In the nave note the pulpit of 1637, covered with delightful and intricate carving. On the wall of the north aisle is the Royal Arms of James II, in cast iron, of 1687, a very rare feature.

At the west end is the plain stone font, reputed to be 14th century; and facing each other on the walls above, monuments to Octavia Lady Ellenborough, sister of Lord Castlereagh, a kneeling woman by Sir Francis Chantrey 1821; and Elizabeth Buggins 1659, a splendid large classical architectural tablet of black and white marble.

In the vestry at the west end is a monument to the brewer William Wiffin and his wife Helen 1652, a tablet with a pediment.

The **churchyard** is largely surrounded by the 18th century kitchen garden walls of North Cray Place, which also extend along St James Way. To the west of the church is a magnificent iron gate, also 18th century, which led to North Cray Place itself; from the gate, another path leads down to the Five Arch Bridge *(see Footscray 17A)*.

There are some interesting memorials in the churchyard: to the south, the memorial to Frances Madocks 1790 with a large Portland stone vase, and tombstones to members of the Vansittart family; and to the east, two adjoining Portland stone chest tombs 1701 with fine heraldic carving to the Frith family, and alongside, the Moberley tomb 1948 with curly cross and heraldic carving.

In Parsonage Lane is another burial ground for the church, set up in the 1940s.

**4. 166/170 North Cray Road.** This is an interesting group of houses:

**No 168 (Old School) & no 170 (School House)** were the former **North Cray National School**, built 1860 and used as a school until 1959. No 168 was the school itself, and no 170 the schoolmaster's house. They are a strange pair, of red brick with a fine steep roof, no 168 with Gothic doors and windows. No 170 bears a cartouche: 'This school and schoolhouse with the adjacent grounds were a free gift to the parish of North Cray by Western Wood of North Cray Place'; the tablet is of 1863 and commemorates his death.

**No 166 (Pear Tree Cottage).** A fine building, of pink-painted brick, with a plaque reading '1790' on the front. There are substantial rear extensions, and it is situated in large grounds. There is a fanciful iron porch, which is probably early 19th century.

**5. *Rose Cottage**, 152/4 North Cray Road. A highly attractive pair of timber-framed cottages, formerly part of a longer terrace and now converted to one house. Probably basically 16th or 17th century, though much altered and restored. Note the unusual window in the shape of a concave diamond.

6. Site of the **medieval hall-house. This house, known locally as Woodbine Cottage, was opposite nos 152/4 on the rural lane which was North Cray Road until 1968; it was in the middle of the proposed dual carriageway, so was dismantled and in 1978 re-erected amongst other 'rescued' buildings at the Weald & Downland Open Air Museum at Singleton, just north of Chichester, West Sussex.

*The Museum is open 1st March to 31st October, daily 1100-1700; 1st November to 28th February, Wednesdays & Sundays, & 26th January to 2nd January daily, 1100-1600. Admission charge.*

The Museum has restored it to its conjectured original condition as an early 15th century hall-house, having removed its weatherboarded and brick facing, its chimneys and later internal partitions.

It has been given a prominent position in the Museum, near the entrance, and appears as a timber-framed house, jettied to the side, with the external timbers painted red. It consists of a central full-height open hall, with a two-storey service wing to the left and a two-storey solar wing to the right.

One enters directly into the hall. To the left are two doorways, one into the buttery, and the other into the pantry, with stairs leading to a chamber above. To the right, behind the high table, are also two doorways, one to a staircase leading up to the solar (or main bed-sitting room) and the other into a parlour below.

7. The White Cross. A fine early 19th century brick pub, with a white cross over the central doorway. The modern extension to the south is well designed and reminiscent of a coach-house.

8. *Loring Hall. A fine stuccoed mansion, formerly called Woollett Hall, now a nursing home. The central part with its bold porch is c1760, with later extensions on both sides. A high brick wall in front makes it impossible to see, but there are good views of the frontage by going a short way up the entrance drive to the right, and also from the car park of The White Cross.

A blue plaque on the front wall by the entrance reads: 'Viscount Castlereagh 1769-1822 statesman lived and died here'. Another plaque a short way up the entrance drive reads: 'Here lived from 1811 to 1822 Robert Stuart Viscount Castlereagh, 2nd Marquess of Londonderry, Foreign Secretary from 1812 to 1822; from 1812 to 1815 he negotiated treaties which gave peace to Europe, in North America his settlements led to the demilitarised frontier between Canada and the USA'.

On the right of the entrance drive is the Lodge, probably mid 19th century, and at the rear, hard up against the north wall, is the stable block, which is basically late 19th century though much altered and extended.

The sports ground at the rear (as well as the stable block) is used by Goldsmiths College. This area gives a good view of the rear of the mansion, with its central canted bay and large balustraded terrace; the tower at the northern end was added in the late 19th century.

Water Lane runs alongside the high brick north wall, which is probably 19th century though restored. The wall precludes any views until you reach the end by the bridge over the River Cray, and from here there is another view of the rear.

**9. Vale Mascal**, 128 North Cray Road. This house of 1746 is impossible to see properly behind its high front wall and hedges, though the view is somewhat better from the other side of the main road. The view is of the upper floor only, and of a Gothic style doorway in the front wall, which leads by a short glazed covered way to the ground floor entrance.

It was originally a much larger house, built as part of the Mount Mascal Estate *(see 11)*. A top floor was removed, as well as a whole section to the south, in the 1950s.

The house presents its best aspect at the rear, where the grounds embrace a section of the River Cray, with its own boat-shaped island. Here the house and its surroundings are strikingly beautiful, but this cannot be viewed from any point accessible to the public.

To the south is **Vale Mascal Court**, 130/2 North Cray Road, which was the old coach-house and stables, 19th century, nicely restored. Beyond that is **Oak Cottage,** 136 North Cray Road, which was a pair of estate cottages, late 19th century but much restored.

The grounds of the house originally covered a much larger area, and were landscaped around the river, with lakes, islands and channels, cascades and weirs, in a way which was considered quite remarkable at the time. Some flavour of the beauty of the landscaping can be gained from the open area to the north; and of the ingenuity of the scheme from the grounds of 112 North Cray Road, where the Gothic bath-house *(see below)* is located.

**10.** The **\*\*Gothic bath-house**. This curious chapel-like building of c1766 (restored in 1990), situated in lovely surroundings by the east bank of the River Cray, used to be in the grounds of Vale Mascal. It is now at the end of the long garden of 112 North Cray Road, which is a house of the late 1930s. Such bath-houses were not rare in the 18th century, but very few now remain.

> Although 112 North Cray Road is a private house, the bath-house can be viewed by the public from 1300 hours on the first Sunday of each month from May to September. Persons wishing to visit the bath-house on these days should telephone Mrs Frances Chu in advance on 0322 554894 to confirm the date. Those with a special interest who wish to visit on another date should telephone Mrs Chu to ask whether a special arrangement can be made.

At this point the River Cray has two subsidiary channels, one of which feeds into the bath-house with an outfall to the river, the water flow being controlled by a sluice gate inside the bath-house.

The building is mainly of flint, with a chimneystack and a tiled roof, and is gabled on all four sides. The entrance doorway is under the chimneystack. The other sides have Gothic-style windows; there are also a number of tiny round-headed and diamond-shaped windows, all blind.

Inside a four foot deep L-shaped plunge-bath occupies most of the space, but there is also a small corner fireplace and a stone platform, and the wooden sluice-gate, all under a vaulted ceiling.

**11. Avenue Lodge**, 37 North Cray Road. This was one of the lodges for **Mount Mascal**; it is a strange building with a circular tiled roof and Gothick windows, probably c1840. (Another lodge, which retains its original thatched roof, is at 107 Tile Kiln Lane - *see Bexley 80*.)

> Mount Mascal was a large 17th century mansion situated on a slope to the east of North Cray Road. Its estate was vast, extending east to cover much of Joydens Wood and west to the River Cray, and included the grounds of Vale Mascal *(see 9, 10)*; it began to be broken up from the early 19th century onwards. The remaining parts of the estate were sold and the mansion demolished in 1957.

A lane near the lodge leads uphill (note the avenue of trees to the right) to the site of Mount Mascal, now occupied by **Jaquets Court (11A)** of 1957. Beyond is Home Close Farm; it incorporates some former outbuildings of Mount Mascal, though substantially altered and transformed, and most of the farm buildings are postwar.

A public footpath, part of the Cray Riverway, leads from opposite Water Lane past Home Close Farm to Mount Mascal Stables, which are postwar - the Keepers Cottage of Joydens Wood is nearby *(see Bexley 82A)*. It is a very rural track, which can become very muddy in places, and involves negotiating a stile. The public footpath leads on via a National Grid road to Dartford Road.

**12. Dower House**, 85 North Cray Road. A large imposing L-shaped house, with its entrance at the central angle. The original part, late 18th century but modified c1820, is parallel with the road; the west wing was added later in the 19th century, when the entrance was moved from the rear.

The building in the corner adjoining the road is the old coach-house, basically mid 19th century, but considerably altered and enlarged.

**13. The Red House**, Bunkers Hill. A pleasant mid 19th century house of deep red brick, with odd Gothick windows. It was formerly part of the Mount Mascal estate.

**14. Little Mascal Farm**, at the junction of Bunkers Hill and Cocksure Lane. An interesting complex, many of the older farm buildings having been retained. If the gates are open, an early 19th century weatherboarded **granary** on staddlestones *(see also Bexley 1, page 18)* can be seen immediately to the right, and the rear of the old stables can be seen ahead.

Ask permission to go further into the site. To the left is the 19th century farmhouse, with a modern porch. Beyond the stables can be seen an old cow-shelter and, to the right, an old barn.

**15. The White House**, Cocksure Lane. An attractive mid 18th century house, which may conceal a 17th century structure.

**16. Manor Cottages**, 53/59 Parsonage Lane. This terrace of two-storied weatherboarded cottages, probably mid 19th century, is in totally rural surroundings.

Opposite these cottages is **Gattons Plantation (16A)**, a small area of very dense woodland, owned by The Woodland Trust; because of the dense undergrowth the Trust does not consider it suitable for visitors.

Parsonage Lane continues as a narrow lane, and becomes a pleasant woodland footpath. Joydens Wood (with one of its pedestrian entrances) is on the left *(see Bexley 82)*, and Chalk Wood *(see below)* is on the right.

**17. Chalk Wood** is a belt of woodland managed by the London Borough of Bexley. It is a continuation southwards of Joydens Wood, though not so extensive.

**18. 1/3 Parsonage Lane.** Originally three cottages of 1892, but it looks like a large and unified house, with a tile-hung upper floor. Note on the side the initials RAV (Robert Arnold Vansittart, who owned Foots Cray Place and North Cray Place at the time).

**19. Gattons**, 8 Parsonage Lane. A pleasing mid 19th century white building.

**20. *Cray Hall**, 141 North Cray Road. An attractive low stuccoed building c1830, formerly called Honeyden, set back from and rather difficult to see from the main road. However, a lane leads round to the south which gives a good view. Note the ornamental entrance porch with its tented canopy, and a similar verandah to the south. To the rear the surroundings are totally rural.

The original lodge is now on the other side of North Cray Road, at 77 St James Way *(see 1)*.

**21. Ruxley Cottage**, Maidstone Road. A large white-washed house on the roundabout, probably mid 19th century, with a castellated porch and fanciful bargeboarding.

**22. Tollgate**, Maidstone Road. A small white-washed house, probably early 19th century, originally a tollgate cottage on the London to Maidstone road.

**23. Ruxley Manor Garden Centre.** This large commercial complex stands on a magnificent sloping site, with panoramic views over North Cray and Joydens Wood to the north. It contains two interesting older buildings - Ruxley Manor Farmhouse and St Botolphs Church.

> Ruxley (previously called Rokesle) was once a village. The Manor was given by Henry VIII to his archbishop Thomas Cromwell in the early 16th century, and the present farmhouse is thought to stand on the site of the Manor House.
> The old church has been there since the 12th century, though excavations in 1968 revealed the footings of an even earlier church on the site. It was deconsecrated in 1557, after the parish of Ruxley was united with the parish of North Cray, and was subsequently used as a barn.

***Ruxley Manor Farmhouse (23A)**, on the right of the entrance drive, is an attractive building, probably late 18th century, with a 19th century extension to the right.

***St Botolphs Church (23B)** is opposite, a church with single cell rectangular plan, ie without structural division between nave and chancel. The walls are of flint and rubble, probably late 12th century, and the doorway and windows are 13th century. Though at present a ruin, it is in the course of restoration.

Depending on the building work, the interior can be accessed through a gap on the southern side, though extreme care should be taken; note the twin sedilia and piscina at the eastern end, which are 13th century and quite well preserved.

Adjoining the church to the east is the substantial stump of an old oasthouse.

Beyond the entrance to the main garden centre, the 19th century **coach-house** has been converted to a restaurant.

Nearby is a recently imported **K2 type red cast-iron telephone kiosk**, designed by Sir Giles Gilbert Scott in 1927. (It is distinguishable from the later K6 type in that all panes of glass are the same size.)

# Notes on some Architects & Artists

(Gazetteer references - B = Bexley, BH = Bexleyheath, W = Welling, S = Sidcup, F = Footscray, NC = North Cray)

**Frank Atkinson**, 1869-1923 *(F16)*. An Edwardian baroque architect, a disciple of Norman Shaw. He designed Bromley Town Hall, and the Waring & Gillow store.

**George Baines** *(B 49; S 29)*. An architect who specialised in non-conformist churches in the late Victorian period.

**Lancelot 'Capability' Brown**, 1716-83 *(F 17; NC 3)*. Architect and landscape gardener, pioneer of the 'picturesque landscape'. His designs were in the grand manner, often involving creation of great lakes and lawns, and planting belts of trees. He 'improved' numerous country estates; his most famous work was at Blenheim Palace.

**Sir Edward Burne-Jones**, 1833-98 *(BH 39)*. Leading artist of the Pre-Raphaelite movement, and close associate of William Morris. His favourite subjects were medieval and romantic legends, often portrayed in a rather melancholy style. His stained glass can be seen in many churches and cathedrals.

**Sir William Chambers**, 1723-96 *(W 8, 9)*. A Palladian architect, whose work included Somerset House and The Albany. In his earlier years he designed several buildings in a Chinese style, including the pagodas at Kew Gardens and at Blackheath.

**Basil Champneys**, 1842-1935 *(B 24, 25)*. A leading architect in both Victorian Gothic and Queen Anne styles. He designed the Indian Institute, Oxford; Newnham College, Cambridge; and John Rylands Library, Manchester.

**Sir Francis Chantrey**, 1781-1841 *(NC 3)*. Outstanding and prolific sculptor of the Georgian period. His works included the statues of George IV in Trafalgar Square, the Duke of Wellington at the Royal Exchange, and William Pitt in Hanover Square.

**Ewan Christian**, 1814-95 *(BH 11; S 53)*. Architectural adviser to the Ecclesiastical Commissioners from 1850. In addition to many churches, he designed the National Portrait Gallery.

**Sir Ninian Comper**, 1864-1960 *(S 11)*. He specialised in church monuments, and also designed and restored many churches.

**Kenneth Dalgleish**, 1887-1964 *(S 7, 32, 43)*. A distinctive architect of the Sidcup area, who designed The Woodman pub and Old Forge Way.

**Thomas Dinwiddy**, 1845-c1926 *(S 46)*. An architect of South-East London. He designed the Laurie Grove Baths, New Cross; the Roan School for Girls, Greenwich; The Hollies, Sidcup; and Grove Park Hospital.

**Hans Feibusch** *(W 16)*. German-born mural painter who settled in London in the 1930s. He has done murals in many postwar church buildings and restorations in South London.

**Fitzroy Robinson & Partners** *(BH 33)*. A partnership specialising in major office and retail complexes, whose many works include the Whitgift Centre, Croydon; the Broadway Centre, Bexleyheath; Lloyds Computer Building, Southwark; Rothschilds, New Court.

**John Flaxman**, 1755-1826 *(S 13)*. One of the leading classical sculptors of his time, and a prolific sculptor of monuments, which are in St Pauls Cathedral, Westminster Abbey, and many Central London and suburban churches.

**Thomas Ford** *(W 13, 16)*. An architect who has since the war built many churches and carried out many restorations, often with rather startling interiors, in South London.

**John Gibson**, 1791-1866 *(S 13)*. A sculptor in the classical style, who worked closely with John Flaxman. He lived in Rome for most of his adult life.

**GMW** (Gollins Melvin Ward & Partners) *(F 3)*. A prestigious partnership, whose major works in the London area include the new Covent Garden, Nine Elms; the Commercial Union and P & O buildings, Leadenhall Street; Castrol House, Marylebone Road; and Sidcup Technology Centre.

**William Habershon**, 1818-92 *(BH 9)*. One of a distinguished architectural family, who worked from 1860 to 1878 in partnership with **Alfred Pite** (1832-1911). They worked mainly in a classical style, in reaction to the prevailing Gothic.

**Henry Hakewill**, 1811-80 *(F 13)*. A prolific builder and restorer of churches, in both Gothic and classical styles.

**Sir Edward Maufe** *(B 10)*. A traditional yet eclectic modern architect, whose works have included Guildford Cathedral and some distinctive London churches - St Thomas, Hanwell; St Saviour, Acton; and St Columba, Pont Street. He lived at The Red House in the interwar period.

**William Morris**, 1834-96 *(BH 39)*. Designer of textiles, wallpaper and furniture; poet, whose principal works were based on Norse mythology and Icelandic sagas; early socialist activist, and pioneering writer on socialism. He was an advocate of craftsmanship, as a reaction to Victorian capitalist mass-production. His design work can be seen in the Victoria and Albert Museum; the William Morris Gallery at his childhood home at Walthamstow; Kelmscott Manor, Oxfordshire; and The Red House, Bexleyheath.

**George Fellowes Prynne**, 1853-1927 *(S 11)*. An important architect in the Gothic style, who worked mostly on church building and restoration. He is noted for his chancel screens.

**Sir Giles Gilbert Scott**, 1880-1960 *(B 3, 16; NC 23)*. Architect of Liverpool Anglican Cathedral, Battersea Power Station and Waterloo Bridge; and designer of the old red cast-iron telephone kiosks.

## 92 - ARCHITECTS & ARTISTS

**John Shaw**, 1803-70 *(S 50)*. A distinctive architect in the classical style, whose main works were colleges, including Goldsmiths College and Wellington College.

**Hieromonk Sophrony** *(W 15)*. A monk of the Russian Orthodox Church, and a noted modern iconographer.

**Joseph Tall** *(BH 16)*. A Victorian pioneer of the use of concrete in building

**Sir Robert Taylor**, 1714–88 *(W 8, 9)*. The leading Palladian architect of the 1750-70 period; he radically adapted Palladian models, with the central staircase being the central feature of his interiors, and the canted bay window a favourite design feature. His work included Asgill House at Richmond, Stone Buildings at Lincolns Inn, and Danson Mansion.

**Wallis Gilbert** & Partners *(F 1)*. A leading practice of the 1930s, specialising in 'art deco' style factories. Their works included the Hoover factory at Perivale, Wrigley at Wembley, and Glaxo at Greenford, as well as Victoria Coach Station.

**Isaac Ware**, 1700-1766 *(F 16)*. Leading Georgian architect in the Palladian style. He designed the beautiful south wing of the Rangers House on Blackheath.

**Philip Webb**, 1831-1915 *(BH 39)*. He is considered the pioneer architect of the Arts & Crafts movement, and worked closely with William Morris. His principal houses, like Standen and The Red House, were in a vernacular style.

# BIBLIOGRAPHY

(including books and publications consulted, and books recommended for further reading, especially for information on local history and architectural detail.)

*London 2: South,* by Bridget Cherry & Nikolaus Pevsner, with section on Bexley by John Newman (Buildings of England series; Penguin Books, 1983)
*Handbook to the Environs of London,* by James Thorne (1876, republished 1970)
*The Industrial Archaeology of South East London* (Goldsmiths College Industrial Archaeology Group, 1982)
*Lewisham to Dartford via Bexleyheath and Sidcup,* by Vic Mitchell & Keith Smith (London Suburban Railways, Middleton Press 1991)
*Borough Walks,* both old and new series (Bexley Civic Society)
*Old Ordnance Survey Maps,* published by Alan Godfrey - Bexleyheath 1862, Bexley 1870, Lamorbey 1895, Sidcup 1908
*The Archaeology of the Bexley Area,* by P. J. Tester (Bexley Libraries 1985)
*Hall Place, Bexley,* by P. E. Morris (Bexley Libraries 1970)
*Hall Place, a short history & guide,* by J. C. M. Shaw & Mick Scott (Bexley Libraries 1989)
*Bexley Village,* by P. J. Tester (Bexley Libraries 1987)
*A History of St Marys Church Bexley,* by Miss K. M. Roome (1974)
*Bexley Deneholes,* by R F Le Gear (Bexley Libraries 1992)
*A Walk around Joydens Wood* (The Woodland Trust)
*The Bexleyheath Phenomenon,* by J. C. M. Shaw (Bexley Libraries 1983)
*The Red House,* by Edward Hollamby (Architecture Design & Technology Press 1991)
*East Wickham & Welling,* by P. J. Tester (Bexley Libraries 1979)
*The History of Danson,* by Ruth Hutcherson (Bexley Libraries 1985)
*The Roman Settlement at Welling,* by Derek Garrod and Brian Philp (Kent Archaeological Rescue Unit 1992)
*The Sidcup Story,* by John Mercer (Bexley Libraries 1988)
*A History of St John the Evangelist, Sidcup,* by John Mercer (1989)
*Holy Trinity Lamorbey,* a Parish History
*Blackfen,* by Susan Ilott (Bexley Libraries 1977)
*Foots Cray,* by Gertrude Nunns (Bexley Libraries 1982)
*All Saints Church, Foots Cray* , a history (1988)
*St James Church, North Cray,* a picture guide by F. Drake & Venn Sturton (1970)

All the above publications, and of course many more books, maps and documents, can be consulted at the **Bexley Local Studies Centre**, Hall Place, Bourne Road, Bexley (phone 0322 526574).

# INDEX

(Gazetteer references - B = Bexley, BH = Bexleyheath, W = Welling, S = Sidcup, F = Footscray, NC = North Cray)

### Churches etc
All Saints - F 13
Bethany Hall - BH 17
Bexley Hospital Chapel - B 76A
Blendon Methodist - B 66
Christ Church Bexleyheath- BH 11
Christ Church Sidcup - S 25
Christ the Saviour - W 12
Days Lane Baptist - S 40
Footscray Baptist - F 9
Good Shepherd - S 41
Holy Redeemer - S 37
Holy Trinity - S 53
Old Bexley Baptist - B 9
St Andrew - B 75
St Barnabas - B 81
St Botolphs - NC 23B
St James - NC 3
St James the Great - B 67
St John the Evangelist Bexley - B 52
St John the Evangelist Sidcup - S 11
St John the Evangelist Welling - W 7
St John Fisher - B 6
St Lawrence of Canterbury - S 26
St Mary Bexley- B 24 -25
St Mary the Virgin Welling - W 16
St Michaels - W 13
Sidcup Community - S 29
Trinity Chapel - BH 9
United Reformed Bexley - B 48
United Reformed Bexleyheath - BH 18
War Memorial Garden - BH 10
Welling Methodist - W 2

### Housing developments
Albany Park Estate - B 74
Clarendon Mews - B 38
Cottage Field Close - B 72
Falconwood Park Estate - W 1
Foresters Homes - BH 19
Hogs Hole Cottages - BH 40
The Hollies - S 46
Jaquets Court - NC 11A
Marlborough Park Estate - S 44
Maypole - B 78
Montrose Park Estate - S 52
Old Forge Way - S 7

St Marys Home - B 33
Stylemans Almshouses - B 4
Thomas Shearley Court - B 20
Ursula Lodges - S 8
Victoria Homes - B 11

### Industrial archaeology
Albany Park Station - B 74
ASDA - BH 13
Bexley Bridge - B 21
Bexley Station - B 3
Bexley Workhouse - B 46
Bexleyheath Station - BH 1
Bowls Pavilion - F 16A
Broadway Shopping Centre - BH 33
Cannon Cinema - S 9B
Clock Tower - BH 32
Coal duty markers - B 79, 81
Concrete churches - B 66; S 37
Concrete houses - BH 16
East Wickham Farm - W 14
Electricity generating station - B 16A
Falconwood Station - W 1
Finger signs - B 17
Fire-engine shed - B 23
Five Arch Bridge - F 17A
Footscray Bridge - F 4
Gothic bath-house - NC 10
Granaries - B 1A; NC 14
Kent Brewery - B 16, 19
Klinger Works - F 1
Kwik Save - BH 12
Lamorbey Baths - S 33
Little Mascal Farm - NC 14
Mill Row - B 41
Old mills - B 1A, 40; F 3
Pillar boxes - B 53; S 18
Reffells Brewery - B 14
Russian gun - W 5
Sidcup Station - S 1
Sidcup Technology Centre - F 3
Telephone kiosks - B 3, 15; NC 23
Tollgate - NC 22
Water towers - B 14, 76; S 46
Welling Station - W 4
Woolwich Building Society - BH 22

94

# INDEX - 95

## Listed buildings - Grades 1, 2* only
All Saints Church - F 13
Christ the Saviour Church - W 12
Danson Mansion - W 9
Danson Stables - W 9A
Frognal - S 15
Gothic bath-house - NC 10
Hall Place - B 1
Red House - BH 39
St Marys Church - B 24

## Parks, woods, open spaces
Beverley Wood - S 38
Bexley Woods - B 59
Bexleyheath Cemetery - BH 11A
Chalk Wood - NC 17
Churchfield Wood - B 28
Cray Riverway - F 17
Danson Park - W 8
Fair Field - B 49
Footscray Meadows - F 16-17; NC 3
Gattons Plantation - NC 16A
The Glade - S 51
Hollyoak Wood Park - S 39
Joydens Wood - B 82; NC 16
Lamorbey Park - S 51
Rutland Shaw - B 73A
St Marys Cemetery - B 26E
Shoulder of Mutton Green - W 15
Shuttle Riverway - B 58-59, 70; S 39
Sidcup Cemetery - B 73
Sidcup Green - S 16
The Warren - BH 28

## People
At-Hall family - B 1
Sir Robert Austen - B 1, 24
Berens family - S 8, 13
John & Maud de Bladigdone - B 65; W 13
Ursula Bloom - S 50
John Boyd - W 8
Henry Castilayn - B 24, 65
Lord Castlereagh - NC 3, 8
Sir John Champneis - B 1, 24
Bourchier Cleeve - F 16
Dashwood family - B 1, 24
Countess of Limerick - B 1
John Malcolm - S 48, 50, 53
Sir Hiram Maxim - B 77
William Morris - BH 39
David Orme - S 50
Payne family - B 25; W 13
Sir John Pender - F 13
William Pincott - BH 11
Lady Mary Scott - B 65
William Steele - S 50
John Styleman - B 4, 24; W 8
Lord Sydney - S 15
John & Catharina Thorpe - B 23, 24, 25

Vansittart family - F 8, 16; NC 1A, 3, 18
Walsingham family - page 58
Lord Waring - F 16
Sir Philip Warwick - S 15

## Public buildings (present & former)
Bexley Hospital - B 76
Bexley Village Library - B 10
Civic Offices - BH 30
Freemantle Hall - B 7
Frognal - S 15
Hurst Place - B 71
Loring Hall - NC 8
Manor House - S 17
Queen Marys Hospital - S 14
Sidcup Fire Station - S 23
Sidcup Place - S 13
Sidcup Police Station - S 27
Upton Day Hospital - BH 42

## Pubs
Albany - B 74
Alma - S 2
Black Horse Bexley - B 13
Black Horse Sidcup- S 9A
Black Prince - B 2
Coach & Horses - B 34
Crook Log - BH 3
Duke of Edinburgh - BH 30
George - B 43
Golden Lion - BH 5
Jacobean Barn - B 1A
Jolly Millers - BH 21
Kings Arms - BH 34
Kings Head - B 8
Millers Arms - B 18
Moon & Sixpence - W 3
Olde Black Horse - S 36
Old Mill - B 40
Polo Bar - BH 4
Prince Albert - BH 29
Railway Tavern - B 45
Red Lion - F 7
Rising Sun - B 32
Robin Hood & Little John - BH 35
Rose & Crown - W 6
Royal Oak - BH 38
Royal Standard - BH 34
Seven Stars - F 5
Three Blackbirds - B 64
Volunteer - BH 7
White Cross - NC 7
Woodman - S 43

## Schools (incl former) & Colleges
Bexley Music Centre - S 28
Bexley National School - B 12
Bexleyheath National School - BH 14
Bridgen National School - B 62
Burnt Oak - S 47

Doreen Bird College - S 4
Fosters School - W 11
Harenc School - F 12
Holy Trinity - S 49
Lamorbey House - S 50
Lamorbey National School - S 48, 53A
North Cray National School - NC 4
Sidcup National School - S 4
Upland School - BH 8

## Streets

Alma Road - S 2
Arcadian Avenue - B 61
The Avenue - B 69
Avenue Road - BH 2
Bellegrove Road - W 2-3
Bexley High Street - B 3-8, 17-23, 37-47, 51
Blackfen Road - W 10; S 41-43
Bladindon Drive - B 68
Blendon Road - B 62-65
Bourne Road - B 1-2, 9-16
Braundton Avenue - S 45A
Bridgen Road - B 60
Broadway - BH 5, 9, 11-13, 29-34
Broomfield Road - BH 27-28
Bunkers Hill - NC 13-14
Burnt Oak Lane - S 47-49
Carlton Road - S 19
Church Road Bexleyheath - BH 6-8
Church Road Sidcup - S 10
Cocksure Lane - NC 14-15
Crook Log - BH 3-4
Crombie Road - S 45B
Cross Lane - B 57
Dartford Road - B 30-31
Days Lane - S 37, 39-40
Footscray High Street - F 5-7
The Green - S 12, 17
Halfway Street - S 34-36
Hatherley Road - S 3
Hill Crescent - B 29
Hurst Road - B 48, 71; S 51A, 52-53
Lewin Road - BH 37
Lion Road - BH 34-36
Longlands Road - S 45D
Maidstone Road - F 2-3; NC 21-23
Main Road - S 20-26
Manor Road - B 26
Mayplace Road West - BH 20-21
Mount Road - BH 38
North Cray Road - B 27, 34-37; NC 3-12, 20
Old Farm Avenue - S 45C
The Park - S 18
Parkhurst Road - B 53-55
Parkview Road - B 50, 52
Parsonage Lane - NC 16, 18-19
Rectory Lane - S 6; F 10-13
Red House Lane - BH 39-40
Riverdale Road - B 58
Robin Hood Lane - BH 37

St James Way - NC 1-3
Sidcup High Street - S 9
Sidcup Hill - S 8; F 8-9
Station Road - S 28-33
Tile Kiln Lane - B 80-81
Upper Wickham Lane - W 11-13
Upton Road - BH 40-42
Upton Road South - B 56
Vicarage Road - B 32-33
Watling Street - BH 23-26
Welling High Street - W 5-6
Wickham Street - W 14-16
Willersley Avenue - S 45
Woolwich Road - BH 15-16